MINIMALISM FOR FAMILIES

For Families Who Want More Joy, Health, and Creativity In Their Life by Decluttering Their Home, Learning Simple and Practical Budgeting Strategies to Save Money & Worry Less!

By Jenifer Scott

© Copyright 2019 by: Jenifer Scott- All rights reserved.

This book is provided with the sole purpose of providing relevant information on a specific topic for which every reasonable effort has been made to ensure that it is both accurate and reasonable. Nevertheless, by purchasing this book you consent to the fact that the author, as well as the publisher, are in no way experts on the topics contained herein, regardless of any claims as such that may be made within. As such, any suggestions or recommendations that are made within are done so purely for entertainment value. It is recommended that you always consult a professional prior to undertaking any of the advice or techniques discussed within.

This is a legally binding declaration that is considered both valid and fair by both the Committee of Publishers Association and the American Bar Association and should be considered as legally binding within the United States.

The reproduction, transmission, and duplication of any of the content found herein, including any specific or extended information will be done as an illegal act regardless of the end form the information ultimately takes. This includes copied versions of the work both physical, digital and audio unless express consent of the Publisher is provided beforehand. Any additional rights reserved.

Furthermore, the information that can be found within the pages described forthwith shall be considered both accurate and truthful when it comes to the recounting of facts. As such, any use, correct or incorrect, of the provided information will render the Publisher free of responsibility as to the actions taken outside of their direct purview. Regardless, there are zero scenarios where the original author or the Publisher can be deemed liable in any fashion for any damages or hardships that may result from any of the information discussed herein. Additionally, the information in the following pages is intended only for informational purposes and should thus be thought of as universal. As befitting its nature, it is presented without assurance regarding its prolonged validity or interim quality. Trademarks that are mentioned are done without written consent and can in no way be considered an endorsement from the trademark holder.

TABLE OF CONTENT

Introduction 1
Chapter 1 *Definition* 2
Chapter 2 *Mindset Of Minimalism* 8
Chapter 3 *Factors To Consider* 13
Chapter 4 *Things That Clutter* 17
Chapter 5 *Questions To Consider* 21
Chapter 6 *Important Places And Items* 26
Chapter 7 *Furnitures And Other Items* 33
Chapter 8 *Confessions And Steps* 38
Chapter 9 *Decorations And Decluttering* 43
Chapter 10 *Aspects To Embrace* 46
Chapter 11 *Humanity* 51
Chapter 12 *Recap* 55
Chapter 13 *Reasons And Guidelines* 60
Conclusion 66
Description 67

INTRODUCTION

Congratulations on purchasing Minimalism for Families and thank you for doing so.

The following chapters will discuss everything you need to know to develop a mindset of minimalism and build a minimalist lifestyle your entire family can follow. First, we'll talk about what minimalism is and what it can look like in the life of an entire family. We'll go through specific strategies for explaining minimalism to your family members and convincing them to jump on board. We'll talk about methods you can use to declutter your home, as well as specific tips and tricks for each room in your house. Finally, we'll talk about how to deal with family members who remain unconvinced and resistant to your vision of minimalism, as well as how to maintain a lifestyle of minimalism for the long-haul.

Throughout this book, I have tried to provide an easy-to-follow process for developing a minimalist mindset and building a minimalist lifestyle. You can absolutely read through the entire book before taking action, but I designed this book to serve as a guide to walk you through the process. Use this book however you learn best!

I hope this book is extremely practical and useful to you and that it provides you with much-needed encouragement and motivation along the way. As you'll come to see in the following pages, minimalism is an incredibly worthwhile mindset and lifestyle. It will help you and your family learn how to focus on the things that truly matter in your life, like spending more time with each other. It might be a bit painful and difficult at first, but I'm willing to bet that your entire family will eventually come to see the value of it.

As you go through the pages of this book, keep in mind that the guidelines I have written out here are only the opinion of one person. I obviously do not know you or your family. Feel free to take the tips and ideas I've outlined and adjusted it to fit the needs of your family.

There are plenty of books on this subject on the market, so thanks again for choosing this one! Every effort was made to ensure it is full of as much useful information as possible. Please enjoy!

CHAPTER 1
Definition

There's a reason for Walt Whitman's quote, "Simplicity is the glory of expression." In today's busy society of consumerism, with ads running rampant throughout our daily lives, simplicity is something that can be incredibly hard to achieve. We're constantly bombarded with ads, begging us to buy the latest gadgets or the newest upgrade to things we already have. We're tempted by the shiny new toys that promise more happiness, higher status, and ultimately better lives. Our money is constantly being pulled in all different directions, and we're left struggling to make ends meet, looking around and wondering where it all went.

In much the same way, our time is also pulled in different directions, taking our attention off of what's truly important to us and placing it on things that don't matter as much in the long run. As we scurry about from work to soccer practice, to the church, to the gym, to the grocery store, and back home to start the process over again, our lives slip by all too quickly and, once again, we're left standing around, wondering where all the time went.

In such a world, it's hard to see a viable solution. How do you avoid wasting all of your precious time and money on worthless "stuff"? When the whole world is doing one thing, it's extremely difficult to learn how to swim against the tide.

But it can be done!

Simplicity is the cornerstone of the philosophy of minimalism. It means subtracting all of the things that don't add happiness and joy to your life and learning to live with less. It means not trying to fill up all of the empty spaces with trinkets and baubles, even if they're sentimental or valuable. It means saying no a lot so that you can say yes to what really brings you joy.

I don't know what your story is, maybe you just started out in your adult life. Maybe you just got married, and as you merge two people's belongings for the first time, you're finding that you could use a little bit of a trim to cut off a bit of the excess that's starting to build. Or, maybe you're a mom of five, with a large house of your own, a husband, two dogs, and a garage full of unused, outgrown stuff (and an attic...and a basement...), and you find that you spend a lot more time cleaning and taking care of all of that stuff than you do spending time with and taking care of your family.

Whatever end of the spectrum you're on, it's not too late (or too early) to get started on your journey to minimalism!

"But I'm that mom with five kids and ten hundred animals! I've got stuff coming out of my ears! There's no way I'll ever be able to start living a minimalist lifestyle, much less sustain one. Also, my kids would stage a rebellion. Surely it's not possible for me!"

I have to be honest; I'm not exactly where you are. I'm probably somewhere in the middle of the "stuff spectrum." I only have two kids, a husband, and one dog, and my house is about the size of a shoebox. But I promise you, no matter what your life looks like now, living a minimalist lifestyle is absolutely possible. It might take a little bit more work on the front end and a little more intentionality to sustain, but it is possible, and it's absolutely worth the effort.

Before you get down to all of that hard work, though, let me tell you what I mean when I talk about minimalism.

What is minimalism?

To me, minimalism is about trading all of the excess junk that piles up so easily for more of what brings me joy: spending time with my family and friends, writing, sleeping, and experiencing life. It's about teaching my kids to live simple lives so that we can experience the beauty of the world together. It's about working with my husband to build the life we want for our family instead of fighting with him about all of the junk that needs to be taken care of.

For those of you who are new to the idea of minimalism, it's also important to note what minimalism isn't. Minimalism isn't about living like a monk, with absolutely nothing to your name except the clothes on your back and a tiny, windowless room to sleep in. It doesn't even have to be about living in a tiny house and owning just the bare minimum to survive (Although a tiny house might be a great option for you. I know my husband and I are considering it!).

The main idea behind minimalism and the guideline you should hold onto as you work to implement minimalism in your family's life is to figure out what brings you joy and adds value to your life and to let go of anything else.

Minimalism is a mindset and a lifestyle. It's not a project to be completed in a weekend and put back on the shelf for next time. It's a chance to reconsider what your priorities are and to design your life (and your stuff) around those priorities. And although minimalism usually starts by getting rid of excess physical clutter, you'll likely find that it leads to getting rid of all of the clutter in your heart and mind as well.

It's a Trade

Like I said earlier, minimalism isn't about setting unrealistic limits on what you can own. It's about making a trade. Everything costs something, so when you choose to accept something into your life, you're also choosing to let go of something else. When you choose to accept busyness and clutter into your life, you choose to let go of money, time, and experiences. However, you can also choose to let go of the clutter and busyness and welcome back the money, time, and experiences you lost.

It means living intentionally

The process of trimming down all of your stuff naturally leads you to ask questions. Do you really need this knick-knack? Does this bring me joy? By asking yourself these questions, you start to become intentional about what you own and the things you do. It all needs to serve a purpose—the purpose you've set out for yourself and your family.

It means living within your means

When you choose to live a minimalist lifestyle, you learn how to say no to much of the excess you're bombarded by every day. You have the mindset that helps you say no when you're tempted to buy something you probably don't need. Minimalist living means that you live off what you make, and anything extra will just have to wait until you've saved up for it because going into debt to get it isn't an option.

It means learning to tell the difference between a need and a want

Do you really need that new shirt? Does your three-year-old really have to have all of the Paw Patrol dogs and their vehicles? If you have enough shirts to last until laundry day and if your three-year-old has a few beloved toys to entertain him, the answer is no. They are not needs. You might still decide to buy them, but you can do so knowing exactly what you're doing. You're indulging a want—which is not always a bad thing. Minimalism doesn't mean you can never get something you want. What it does mean is that you need to know the difference between a need and a want, and you need to know that you have a place for what you buy. If you indulge in your wants too often, you'll only be building the clutter right back up again.

Advantages of having a minimalist lifestyle

There are so many advantages to minimalism—advantages that go beyond and far deeper than the initial advantage of having a clutter-free home. As I said, minimalism is a trade, a trade of your excess stuff and busyness for more simplicity, deeper relationships, and greater joy. All of these things lead to enormous benefits that you'll be so grateful for at the end of your life that you won't even come close to missing the "stuff" you let go of.

Financial Freedom

As you trim down your belongings and learn to live within your means, you'll find that your money starts to free up as well. You no longer have to buy more and more stuff to "keep up with the Joneses," as it were. You'll be able to get out of debt and live a life full of rich experiences with those you love.

More time

I don't know about you, but even in my shoebox-sized home, I spend an inordinate amount of time cleaning. It feels like I'm constantly picking up toys, vacuuming dog hair, doing laundry, washing dishes, and making beds. And I work, so all of that has to be done outside of my working hours, which is the time I should be spending with my family.
I clean so much because we have too much stuff! Even though we've been on this minimalism journey for a long time now, we're not perfect at it, and in this season of our lives, it's become incredibly difficult to maintain (So, see, you don't have to be perfect at this! I'm writing a book on minimalism, and I'm not perfect at it, either!). My kids have far too many toys (courtesy of well-meaning grandparents who live nearby). I have far too many clothes (courtesy of my recent influx of maternity clothes and subsequent need for clothes that fit my post-baby body). And my husband has far too many hygiene products (courtesy of his strange need to constantly have mousse in his hair and body spray all over his body—even at night. Gotta love him!). We also really love board games, so we have an entire shelf in our closet devoted to all of them.
Needless to say, there's a lot to keep up with, even in my little home. Minimalism can certainly help with that. If my kids had just enough toys to keep them entertained, if I had just enough clothes to last until laundry day, and if my husband had just enough hygiene products to keep himself clean (meaning, only one can of each product instead of five), imagine how much less time I'd have to spend keeping toys organized, folding laundry, and putting hygiene products back in their proper place? That's a lot of time.

Less stress

With less stuff comes less stress. Less time spent cleaning up stuff means more time I could spend on other things that need to get done. Studies have shown (UCLA Center on Everyday Lives and Families 2001-2004) that managing a house full of stuff leads to higher levels of stress and anxiety for mothers. In the study, women associated with a clean and clutter-free home has a successful and happy family.
Excess clutter not only affects mothers but the children as well. Excess stuff means excess stimuli, which leads to greater distraction. Not to

mention, when their mothers are stressed, kids often become stressed as well.

Better relationships

This is a huge one. I know I joke about my husband's surplus of hygiene products, but if I can be honest for a moment, there are days when I want to take his mousse bottle and stab him with the pointy end. The tip might break off before it could do much damage, but the sentiment is still there. In a small house with two very young children, even one excess bottle of mousse out of place makes a room look cluttered and disorganized, which drives me a little crazy.

It drives me crazy because I look at that bottle of mousse, and I know that it's insignificant. It's only one bottle of mousse. But it's one bottle of mousse and one load of laundry and one meal to cook and one pile of toys to put away until it adds up and up and up, and all of my time has gone. It's a maddening reminder of all of the things I have to complete each day just to maintain a livable space (much less a homey and welcoming space), and it stresses me out immensely.

Then, I'm snapping at him and the kids (despite my best efforts to hide my frustration), refusing to tell him what's wrong because, in my mind, he should just know to pick up his own things. My three-year-old is wondering why mommy's upset, and my infant is crying in his chair because I just can't figure out what's going on with him. It's a horrible cycle, and my relationships with my husband, my kids, and even my dog suffers because of it.

Read this carefully: Minimalism is not a magic pill to fix all of your relational ills. In fact, it might initially add conflict that might not have been an issue before (We'll talk about how to handle that in a later chapter.).

However, if you can get over the initial hard work to declutter your home and can consistently build habits to maintain a minimalist lifestyle, it will improve your relationships. You'll have more time to spend with your loved ones. You'll be less stressed about spending that time with them. And you'll be able to experience life with your family in a way that wasn't possible when your home was too cluttered for you to even breathe.

Healthy boundaries

Choosing to live a life of minimalism will mean that you have to say no to some things. Whether it's declining to take on more work for your boss or having a conversation with eager-to-spoil grandparents about the number of toys your children have, maintaining a minimalist lifestyle requires you to develop strong boundaries with those around you. Just remember: setting and enforcing boundaries doesn't make you rude or mean. It means you're honest with others about what you can do and accept. You'll even be able to avoid feelings of resentment toward them that might arise when you do something that violates your boundaries.

So set the boundaries you need to have for your family and be confident in enforcing them. Having boundaries for you and your family is extremely healthy and will make your life with others much more pleasant and honest.

There are so many more benefits to living a minimalist lifestyle that I simply don't have time to go into in this chapter. As you continue reading this book and getting ready to implement minimalism in your family's life, keep these benefits in mind. It can be a long, hard journey (as I've already shared, my family and I are still not perfect at it.), but keeping all of these benefits in mind will give you something to look forward to and motivate you to keep on keeping on.

CHAPTER 2
Mindset Of Minimalism

It might seem ridiculous to think that minimalism can actually work for an entire family—especially one with a couple of young kids. Between all of the sports gear—participating in multiple sports at a time builds character, right? —clothes, school supplies, and toys that constantly pile up, cutting it all down to only the things that are necessary (and keeping it that way) seem an impossible task.

It might be crazy, but the mindset of minimalism is actually most valuable in the context of a family. Minimalism is about replacing all of the clutter that sucks all of your time, money, and energy with the relationships and experiences that really mean the most. And what relationships are more important than family?

None of that takes away from how difficult it can be, though. Believe me; I'm well aware. So how do you get your entire family on board to becoming a minimalist family?

Developing a mindset of minimalism

Most of this book will be about the practical steps you'll take to implement minimalism in your home because the method you use is absolutely important to your success. But understanding and developing a minimalist mindset is every bit as essential to your success. If the steps you take for an example is the car that gets you to your destination, the mindset is the gas that fuels the car; both are necessary if you plan on getting anywhere.

Understand that minimalism isn't just about organizing all of your stuff better and making it look better. Minimalism is about actually reducing the number of possessions you have and getting rid of it all. If you want a book about the organization, this won't be the book for you. This book (and minimalism in general) is about changing your heart and mind in relation to your possessions. It's about developing a mindset that values experiences and relationships more than possessions and that designs a life that reflects those values.

The very first thing you have to do to get started on this journey is developing a mindset of minimalism for yourself. It's hard to convince others to do something you aren't convinced of yourself. If you read the first chapter of this book and found yourself longing for the kind of life described here, you're well on your way to a mindset of minimalism.

Why are you doing this?

One of the first things you need to understand to develop a mindset of minimalism further is why you're doing this in the first place. What is the one reason that stands above all the other good reasons you could have for taking on this journey? What will be the motivator that drives you through the hard times of starting a minimalist lifestyle?

But don't just think about it. Take out a sheet of paper and actually write it down. Start by writing all of the reasons you have for wanting to get rid of all the clutter in your life and home and live a minimalist lifestyle. Then, narrow it down to just one overarching reason. If you want to get really into it, write it down by itself on a sheet of paper and hang it up on your wall or your refrigerator. You can even decorate it if you're into that kind of thing. The point is: to make your reason both extremely important to you and highly visible. That way, when the going gets tough, you can look at the beautiful sheet of paper hanging on your wall and tell the tough to get going. Sorry, my humor is a bit cheesy at times.

What's the purpose of your home?

It's time to take out another sheet of paper. We're doing practical here, folks, not just thoughts swirling around your head. This time, I want you to think about the purpose of your home. What do you want your home to mean to those who step into it? Is it shelter? Is it a place to enjoy friends and family?

Personally, I want my home to be just that: a home. I want it to be somewhere my family and those who visit can go to feel at home. I want it to be calm, beautiful, and comfortable. I want it to be cozy and for people to immediately feel safe there. I want it to be a place where people can be together and experience life together.

If you have the purpose of your entire home written down, start doing the same thing with each room in your home. What is the purpose of your living room? Your kitchen? Your dining space? Your kids' rooms? Your bedroom? For me, I want my living room to be a place for people to relax and spend time together (on super comfy couches). I want my kitchen to be a place where delicious meals are produced that provide nutrition for my family and hospitality for guests. I want my dining space to be a place where people gather to talk about everything and nothing, to connect with each other through conversation and games. I want my kids' rooms to be a place where my kids can go to express themselves through their unique interests and hobbies and to spend a few moments alone when they're feeling overwhelmed. And I want my bedroom to be a place for my husband and me to relax and connect with each other every day.

In short, my home and all of the rooms in it are all about connections, relationships, and experiences.

What purpose do you want your home and its rooms to serve?

What happens next?

Now that you're clear on your own reasons for choosing a minimalist mindset, it's time to start getting into the practical steps you're going to take to start implementing minimalism in your family's life. These first steps are all about bringing your family on board with you and developing a mindset of minimalism within your family as a whole. They're also about becoming more deeply in tune with your underlying desires and purpose in order to cut out the indecision that leads to cluttered homes and lives.

Lead by example

One of the qualities of an effective leader is that they "walk the walk" long before they ever expect anyone else to do it. If you really want to lead a minimalist lifestyle with your family, the first thing you have to do is start minimizing your own stuff. Sometimes it's easy to start minimizing your family members' things. After all, it's all of your kids' toys you have to pick up, or it's all of your husband's (clean) shirts that keep piling your laundry basket high. Your stuff isn't the problem!

Yeah, right. Sorry, sister...or brother. It's easy to see everyone else's stuff and think that's got to go. But if you haven't gotten your family on board yet, that's a sure way to make sure they're never on board. No one likes to wake up one day and find that their belongings are suddenly gone.

However, if you start the process with your own stuff, your family will start to see how you're able to live (happily) with fewer things. They might start asking questions on their own about why you got rid of so much of your stuff. They might even initiate their own "clutter purge" without you having to do much besides answering their questions.

By giving your family members a chance to initiate their own induction into the world of minimalism, you'll be empowering them to take ownership of it. When your entire family is able to take ownership of this new mindset, you'll find that it'll be much easier to sustain a minimalist lifestyle.

Not to mention: if you start the process of minimizing your belongings only with your own stuff, you'll be familiar with the process and able to help your family members get started. The process of minimizing can be a daunting one, so serving as a trailblazer for your family can be a great way not only to get everyone on board but to give them a real-life example to follow.

Hold a family meeting

Once you've been leading your family by example for a little while and have the process down for yourself, it's time to hold a family meeting. In this meeting, share with them your reasons for minimizing your own stuff, as well as the purpose you wrote out for your home. Share why this lifestyle choice is so important to you and how doing it with your own stuff has already changed the way you live. Explain to them what minimalism means to you—and what minimalism does not mean.

If I were you, I'd go into this meeting with notes prepared. It might seem forced and a little bit silly to be so formal about a family meeting, but minimalism can seem like a radical lifestyle choice to those who don't understand it yet. It's important to be prepared to answer any questions your family members ask. It's also important that you're able to explain it in a way that's easy to understand. And if you're like me, writing it out beforehand will make sure you're able to accomplish both goals, even if you get a little flustered.

It's also important to explain it to them in a way that they'll understand and appreciate. If you have young kids (not toddlers or babies, but kids who are old enough to understand what's going on), remind them of how much time they have to spend cleaning their room right now. Remind them of the times they've been grounded because they didn't clean their room when they were asked to. Paint a picture for them of what it would look like if they had fewer toys in their room, fewer clothes in their closet, and less clutter to keep up with. They'd be able to spend more time outside, hanging out with their friends, or participating in the activities they want to be part of. They might balk at the idea of losing their toys, but it probably won't be too hard to persuade them to give it a try. You might even compromise with them by having them put away most of their toys but keeping them in storage for an agreed upon trial period. If they find that they miss their toys at the end of the trial, they can get some of them back. Just make sure that the trial period is a long enough time that they're able to really get into the routine of having less clutter.

Once you've explained what minimalism is and why you think it's important, ask your family members for their input. Answer their questions and concerns, and if they put up a lot of resistance, try to find ways to compromise with them. Minimizing might have to be a long process of weaning your family off their clutter. But that's ok. Remember that this is about enriching your relationships with your family, not causing division and conflict with them. If taking it slower than you'd like is the cost of avoiding division, it's well worth it.

Find a way to motivate them

Once your family has agreed on the extent and timeline of the minimizing process, it'll be time to start decluttering your house. The initial decluttering will likely take several days and lots of decluttering sessions that will likely give your kids a sour taste for the whole idea, even if they initially agreed to it in the family meeting.

So, find ways to make it fun for your entire family. Offer a reward for participating, like taking them out for a special treat after a long day of decluttering. You could even plan a vacation as a reward for your entire family when the entire house has been decluttered. During your decluttering sessions, play upbeat, fun music that will boost everyone's mood and make it a fun time instead of a boring one.

Another trick you might want to use, especially while working with your kids to get rid of their toys, is to focus on what they want to keep instead of what they want to get rid of. Have them put the things they want to keep in a pile, then simply get rid of the rest without making it a big deal. Keep their mind on the positive side of minimizing, and as much as possible, avoid focusing on the things they're losing.

Teach them to think about others

As your kids go through their things, have them consider what they might be able to give away to another kid who needs toys. Let them know that there are kids in their own neighborhoods and towns who don't have any toys to play with. Then, when you get ready to get rid of the toys for good, research where you can take them, so they'll be given to kids who need them and take your kids with you to drop them off. Being able to see where their toys are going and know that their small sacrifice will help someone else is a great way to motivate your kids, as well as teach them to help other people.

Let them choose

As much as possible, let your kids choose what they want to keep, as long as it's within the guidelines you've set in place (more about that in the next chapter). Allowing your kids to make their own choices about what they want to keep will not only earn brownie points for you but will give them a sense of ownership in the process and responsibility for their belongings.

Getting your family on board with minimizing can be difficult, especially when you have kids. It's hard to convince someone to part with their beloved possessions, but if you're prepared to answer their questions, compromise when possible, and find fun ways to motivate them, it'll be a much smoother transition. Part of your preparation should include setting guidelines for the belongings your family chooses to keep, as well as for how your family will treat those belongings, all of which we'll talk about in the next chapter.

CHAPTER 3
Factors To Consider

It's pretty easy (and can even be fun, once you get in the groove of things) to do the physical work of decluttering your house. What's hard is keeping it decluttered once it's all gone and you start to return to a normal routine. School work starts piling in "we might need this someday" folders again, toys start finding their way home via well-meaning grandparents, and various odds and ends seem to slip through the cracks in your front door. In a shopping bag. That you're carrying (but you needed it!).

Coming up with guidelines for your family is probably the most boring part of this whole process, but it's also one of the most important things you can do to make sure that the clutter stays gone. The first and most important guideline you can set for your family is that of gratitude.

Be thankful for what you have

If you choose to have a list of your guidelines out for your entire family to see on a daily basis (which you should do, by the way), the very first one on that list should be this one. I don't know about you, but I have a preschooler who has gotten in a phase where he can be very ungrateful for what he has. My parents bought him a toy one day, and the next day, he tells me that toy's old and he needs a new one. Despite it being somewhat cute in his three-year-old little boy voice, it's also infuriating (As are most things with a stubborn three-year-old, I'm finding—cute but infuriating.).

You wouldn't know it at that moment, but he's actually very good at saying thank you when people do something for him, though. But that's another story.

My point is: I never in a thousand years would have consciously taught my child that kind of behavior. Perhaps I did it in my own behavior sometimes, but I think it's also just a natural inclination we all have. We want to be better, have more, and do cooler things and that drive isn't always a bad thing. It's also what helps us become better people and do better things with our lives.

Left unchecked, though, it can also lead to entitlement, discontentment, and clutter.

So, it's important to teach our kids to be grateful for what they do have so that they're less likely to want to keep getting more and more. One way to start teaching your kids to be thankful is to share your gratitude with each other every day. Whether it's in the morning, at dinner, at bedtime, or some other time, go around to everyone in your family and have them tell one or two things they're thankful for. The trick is that it can't be something generic (my family, my house, my toys, etc.). It has to be specific, and they have to say why they're thankful for it. And of course, this isn't just for your kids. You and your partner should participate, too! We adults can become just as ungrateful and discontent as our kids can, and we need to train ourselves to focus on what we do have as well.

Another way to do this is to change your "I want..." statements to "I have...". Anytime you find yourself, your partner, or your kids saying, "I want...", stop them and have them rephrase it to say, "I have...". If you hear your kid say they want a new toy, have them say something they already have. Or if you hear yourself say, "I want this beautiful new coat," stop yourself and remember the coat you already have. It probably works just as well as it did last year when you were just as excited about it as you are now about this new coat.

Follow the Rule of Replacement

It might not always be possible, but as often as you can, follow the guideline of "one comes in, one goes out." When you're able to remove something from your house every time something else comes in, it's easy to see how this guideline helps keep clutter from piling up again.

Of course, you probably won't be able to do this with everything. You might need two of something for a particular reason. However, you should try to do it as much as possible. For example, you can use this guideline with your kids. Every time they ask for a new toy, have them think about what toy they already have that they would be willing to get rid of to make room for the new one. Doing this will kill two birds with one stone, so to speak. It will help control the clutter that accumulates, and it will also help your kids learn to make wise choices about their belongings. It might turn out that they don't really want that new toy after all.

This also works well for small items, like hair or beauty products. Every time you buy a new set of makeup, throw your old one out. Don't keep both just because your old one has a tiny bit of your favorite color left.

It can be used for your calendar, too. If you or a family member wants to add something to the calendar (an event, a sport, etc.), make that person choose something to get rid of. Of course, their choice should be something that affects them. If your son wants to start playing baseball, he can't choose to get rid of his sister's soccer from the calendar. That wouldn't make any sense. He has to choose something that affects him, like not playing football or swimming with his friends every week. You can't add more hours to the day or days to the week, so instead of piling your calendar full of stuff and finding yourself running around like a chicken with its head cut off and never having time to just be with your family, stick the "one comes in, one goes out" rule with your calendar as much as possible.

Use it or lose it

If it's not being used and it's not adding beauty and meaning to your life, it has no place in your home. Once a month (week, season, whatever works best for your family), take time to evaluate what's being used and what's been sitting on the shelf for a while. If it isn't being used, find a way to get rid of it. Again, giving your unused belongings away is a great way to teach your kids about helping others and being grateful.

For example, as you bring out clothes for a new season, go through them. If you didn't wear it the year before, it's probably safe to get rid of it. So, do. Wield those decluttering shears often and with enthusiasm!

A place for everything and everything in its place

I'm a smidge OCD about this, and I know my husband hates that about me. But honestly, it's how I stopped losing all of my belongings and started actually knowing where everything is (most of the time). It's also a good guideline for maintaining a minimalist lifestyle. If you don't have space for it, it's hard to keep. So, don't try. If you don't have space for it, you probably don't have a need for it.

This guideline can also be used to manage the number of toys your kids have. Designate a space for each child's toys. Anything that fits in that space and doesn't require the owner to solve a jigsaw puzzle every time they need to close the lid (drawer, etc.) can stay. Anything else has to go. That way, he can keep practically anything he wants to keep, as long as it fits within his designated space.

Items used must also be put away

Clean up time! My three-year-old hates it. But if I don't make him do it, his toys litter the floor and create tripping hazards for anyone in the house. It's actually dangerous. My husband also hates this one. Just ask him.

But it's important! And you're not a nag for insisting on it. Well, I guess you can become one, and that's not good either. Again, our goal here is to create fewer sources of conflict, not more. But families do have rules and one of them should be that, at the end of the day, anything that was taken out during the day has to be put away. Everyone is responsible for their own belongings, another time to cultivate that sense of responsibility in your kids.

There are ways to make it a little more fun, though. Make it part of the getting-ready-for-bed routine, a fun family game with a small prize at the end if you have to. One game could be for everyone to gather their own items and race to see who finishes first. The first person to finish receives the small prize (5 minutes extra to stay up, for example). Another game could be to have everyone gather someone else's items. Whoever gathers the most items wins and receives the prize.

Finish what you start

The final guideline I would suggest (though you may come up with different ones for your family) is that any project that gets started must be finished. This is the guideline that points directly at me. I'm horrible about starting a project and then quitting in the middle. I get distracted by a shinier project (I'm ADHD, forgive me!). I run out of time. Whatever the reason is, I almost never finish the projects I start out to complete.

Most of the time, this happens because I start a project off with far too much energy and enthusiasm. My eyes were greedier than they needed to be, and I just got tired, and the project fell to the wayside. Be realistic from the start about how long a project will take and how hard it's going to be. If you go into something expecting that it's going to be hard, you'll be much better prepared mentally, and you'll be able to prepare yourself physically as well by getting a good night's sleep the night before, taking breaks, eating well, etc.

When you're planning to take on a large project (like decluttering your entire house for the first time), it's important to break the project down into manageable chunks. Start small with a single room or even a single closet in that room. This is hard for me because I'm kind of an "all or nothing" kind of person, but that doesn't usually work out, even for me. There's no way I can declutter my entire house in one day, and I'm willing to bet you won't be able to either.

So, start off small. Even if you build to taking on larger tasks as you go, starting small will ensure that you get your projects finished. Finishing projects feels really great, and as you finish more and more, your momentum and motivation to finish will grow as well, allowing you to take on those bigger projects.

Take some time to decide on the guidelines you want to have for your family and introduce them to your family meeting. Keep in mind that your family members might not be so enthusiastic at first, so be patient and willing to compromise if you have to. Also keep in mind, though, that these guidelines are essential to maintaining a minimalist lifestyle and keeping your house decluttered. Compromise where you must, but don't be too willing to bend.

CHAPTER 4
Things That Clutter

I'm sure you've noticed this phenomenon in your own home, so I don't really need to remind you. But in case you haven't noticed, clutter is annoying. It piles up in your home, making it look disorganized and full of junk. Sometimes my house looks like I'm a toy hoarder. It piles up on your calendar, leaving you hurried, harried, and exhausted. And it piles up in your relationships, infringing on your boundaries and leading you to deal with people you have no business dealing with.

Clutter is so annoying because it piles up and steals away your time, energy, and money. Instead of being able to spend it on the things that actually matter to you, you're forced to spend it on all of the tiny little things that constantly add up.

The tricky part about clutter, though, is that we often become so used to it that we don't even realize it's there. It just piles up quietly until one day, you're looking around your house and wondering where in the world it all came from. Then we get the decluttering bug, which might help tone the clutter down for a moment. But for the most part, accumulating clutter is second nature to us and happens almost subconsciously.

When we think about clutter, we usually think about physical clutter, the little odds, and ends that pile up throughout our houses. However, clutter can accumulate in other areas of your life as well.

Clutter on your calendar

Aside from physical clutter, one of the more vexing types of clutter is the clutter that piles up on your calendar. You bite off more than you can chew for your job. You have meetings scheduled through the next 20 years, it seems. Your daughter is in both drama and choir, both of which have performances on the same weekend. Your son is also in choir, but he can't make it to this weekend's performance because he's traveling with the baseball team. He's also on the basketball team. And maybe even in the band. Your partner's job requires him to work odd hours, so you're always trying to coordinate schedules with him. And you have this friend who constantly wants to call and talk for three or four hours at a time.

It's all too easy for your calendar to become cluttered. As your kids grow older, you want them to be involved in things at their school. It's part of the high-school experience, right? But when you add all of that to your already full calendar of work, friends, and other familial obligations, you'll quickly end up with very little time to spend on things that really matter to you.

Clutter in your mind

You might not think about it much, but your mind can become just as cluttered as your house. If you've ever felt like your brain might be turning to mush inside your head, then you've felt the mental exhaustion that comes with having too much clutter floating around in your mind. In some ways, we can't help this. Our minds are constantly working, telling our body what it needs to do, reminding us not to do things that could get us killed, and otherwise performing tasks that are necessary for daily survival.

That's already a lot of stuff, and it never stops, not even when you're asleep. But then you add onto that all of the extras we pour into our minds, and they can quickly become a constant whirlwind of activity. Mental clutter is distracting, keeping us from being able to focus on things that are important to us. And, when we're unable to focus, we're more likely to be thoughtless and hasty in our decisions, leading us to make poor choices that could affect our relationships, our time, our careers, our energy, and other areas of our lives.

Clutter in your relationships

Have you ever kept up a relationship purely out of a sense of duty or obligation? It's that person who is constantly needy, calling you at all hours of the day, sucking up your time and energy for their own needs. Or it's that person who's constantly negative and critical and who makes it difficult for you to be positive when you're around them.

When my husband and I were dating, he had a friendship like this. The guy was a strange person. He was constantly negative and extremely needy. I sometimes felt like my husband had two girlfriends. And one (not me) was a very bad girlfriend! He also hated me because he thought I was a bad influence on my future husband (not true, by the way!). My husband continued being friends with him because he felt bad that this guy didn't have many other friends. Meanwhile, his real girlfriend (me) felt uncomfortable and even felt slightly ignored in favor of the friend. Eventually, my husband did stop allowing his friend to take my place, they drifted apart, and our relationship was better for it.

In trying to be a nice guy, my husband continued a relationship that threatened to harm other relationships that were important to him. It's incredibly easy to do. Once you have a relationship with someone, it's difficult to end it. No one wants to be the person who stops being friends with someone. It's even more difficult when the toxic relationship is with a family member like a parent, a sibling, or even a grown child. However, relationships that do nothing but take up your time and energy and harm the other relationships in your life should be let go, regardless of how hard it is. Perhaps you can keep the door open to renewing the relationship in the future (in the case of close family relationships), but it might be that you need to take a good, long break from them in order to declutter your life of the relationships that are causing you harm.

Clutter in your house

Physical clutter is easily the most visible type of clutter you can have, and interestingly, it's often a sign of how much clutter you have in the other areas of your life. A cluttered house can contribute to a cluttered mind. It can also be a sign of a cluttered calendar and relationships that need to be let go because both will eat up the time you could be spending managing the clutter in your house.

Clutter in your house is all of the stuff that piles up throughout the years, most of which you use once or twice then put away in the garage, never to be used again. It's the clothes you keep because you'll fit into it again, "one day." It's the multiple layers of kids' artwork that covers your refrigerator because each one is precious, and you can't find it in your heart to throw it away. It's the equipment for the sport your child no longer wants to play.

Physical clutter is absolutely the most visible, but it's also probably the easiest to manage, and it can be a first step in learning how to minimize the clutter in all of the other areas of your life.

Decision Fatigue

One of the most damaging results of physical clutter is something called decision fatigue, and it's a type of mental clutter that's directly related to the physical clutter you choose to keep. Decision fatigue is something that happens when you give yourself too many options. For example, when you have a closet full of clothing options, it can actually take you longer to choose something to wear than if your closet only contained the essentials.

Studies have also shown that decision fatigue has an especially damaging effect on kids. It puts their minds on mental overload and leads to all kinds of bad behavior. Having too many options for clothes, food, and yes, even toys, is damaging for kids, so decluttering your home and learning to live a minimalist lifestyle will have huge benefits for your kids, as well as for you.

How to get started with minimalism

Living a minimalist lifestyle is a process, one that takes a lot of work and a lot of patience to start and to maintain. Like with anything, though, the only thing you can do is start with step one and keep taking one step at a time. It might take a long time and a lot of frustration (That's where the patience comes in!), but if you just get in there and get started and continue moving forward, you'll eventually get to where you want to be.

To put it as simply as possible, that first step is to pick one area of your house and just start moving things out. Make it something small: a closet or a bookshelf, maybe. Or if you're more ambitious and have more time on your hands, start with an entire room. Whatever you do, make it something manageable, something you can get done in one session.

Then just start getting rid of stuff. If possible, try to find a good home for it all, like a donation center or a Goodwill. However, if you don't have something like that available to you, don't waste your time trying to find the perfect home for it all. Throw it away or have a bonfire night. We'll talk more about the whole process in the coming chapters, but for now, keep the first step in mind: pick one small, manageable area to get yourself started and get it done in one session.

CHAPTER 5
Questions To Consider

Ok, so clutter is annoying. We agree on that. If you're still reading this book, I assume you are at least intrigued by the idea of minimalism and are curious to see how this whole idea could play out in your own family. You may have even started thinking about the guidelines you want to set for your family and planning the meeting you'll have to get them on board.

That's all well and good, and you're at a great place to get this whole thing going. But how do you actually go about clearing out the overflow of useless stuff piling up in your home? How do you decide what things you want to keep and what you could get rid of? What do you do with the stuff you decide to toss? These are all great questions, and I'm so glad you asked them! We'll be taking a look at all of that in the next several chapters. In this chapter, we'll look at the overall strategies you can use to declutter your home, and in the following chapters, we'll walk through each room in your home, considering the things that probably should stay and the opportunities for minimizing the clutter.

Learning to ask the right questions

One of the first things you'll have to learn in order to start on the journey to minimalism is how to ask the right questions. If you haven't done it already, you should seriously stop reading right now and take a few minutes to consider your reasons for doing this, as well as the purpose you want your family and your home to have. Both of these will inform your answer to pretty much every question you go through in this process, so it's definitely to your advantage to be extremely clear on them.

What questions should you ask?

Remember the first step in the decluttering process? Pick one spot and get it done in one session. Great. Except where do you get started? How do you decide what you should keep in that one spot? Well, you ask a bunch of questions. As you stare at your overflowing closet, catch-all room, or bookshelf, have a list of questions scrolling through your mind. Start pulling things out until it's completely empty, then go through each individual item and seriously consider your answers for that item:

What purpose does this item have?

Everything in your minimalist home should have a specific purpose. There can be little decorations and things to improve the aesthetics of your home, but for the most part, there should be a practical purpose for everything.

Am I currently using it, or will it be used in the coming months?

If you have a future purpose for it, make sure that it will actually be used for a specific purpose. For example, don't keep your too-small clothes because you think you'll be able to fit in them again. By the time that happens, you'll likely want new clothes! A new wardrobe is a great reward for getting to your goal weight, so don't keep a bunch of old stuff that just adds to the clutter! On the other hand, if you're decluttering your garage in the winter and come to your son's baseball gear, certainly don't get rid of all of that! If you plan on registering him for baseball again in the spring, he'll definitely use it again. Perhaps you can get rid of a few of the baseballs or the extra bats and gloves you have lying around that are too small for him. But if it's the right size and he wants to play again, by all means, it should be kept!

Do I have more than one?
No one needs ten empty notebooks (I'm pointing at myself on this one.). Obviously, you should have more than one shirt and pair of pants. However, there are a lot of things in our homes that we could get by with only one. For example, keep only one pair of each type of shoe you need—work, sandals, boots, etc.—instead of accumulating several pairs of each. Or, who needs twenty different wrapping paper designs? Keep one roll for Christmas (maybe two) and one or two for birthdays/generic gifts. If you're minimalists, though, you might not have too many gifts to wrap in the first place, since you'll want to keep your kids' toys to a minimum as well!

Does it simplify my life or complicate it?
My husband is a technology guru. He loves it! And I love it, too! In fact, I'm writing this book on my beautiful MacBook that makes me incredibly happy every time I open it. I know that's goofy and a little materialistic (a lot materialistic), but that's the way it is! Anyway, my husband, though, is kind of obsessed with finding new and unique ways to store and watch our movies. It's great because he's getting a lot of our movies where we can watch without relying on the internet. However, it can also make things quite complicated when it doesn't work the way it's supposed to. One of the questions you should ask yourself about each item is, "Does this make my life easier or more complicated?" Hopefully, when we get it set up correctly, the movie stuff will make life simpler. But for now, it definitely makes it more complicated. If something in your home makes your life more complicated, it might be better just to throw it out.

What do I really need during this period of my life?
This is kind of similar to the second question about if something is being used or not. Again, don't keep your too-small clothes just because you plan to fit into them again someday. Another example would be keeping a curling iron after chopping all of your hair off. Nobody with a pixie cut needs a curling iron, so if you have a haircut like that, throw out the curling iron (Pro tip: no one really needs a curling iron at all. A thinner (1" or so) flat iron can actually curl hair beautifully!)!

Could I borrow it?

If you use a particular item, but only on very rare occasions, is it possible that you could borrow it from someone else who has that item? For example, if you almost never use your kitchen aid, but you have a friend who has one, could you find a new home for yours and borrow your friend's on the rare occasions you want to use it?

Do I want to leave this for my family?

This question could be interpreted in one of two ways. On items that are more sentimental in value, you should consider if it's something you would want to pass down to your kids or their kids someday when you're gone. Things like family heirlooms or particularly special clothes or blankets might mean something to your family members after you pass away. On the flip side of this question, one of the less romantic aspects of leaving things for your family is that when you pass away, someone is going to have to figure out what to do with everything you own. When my grandfather passed away, bless his heart, it was a job to clear out his and my grandmother's home because they had accumulated so much stuff! So, as you consider each item, you might also think about your kids: is it important enough to keep that if you passed away suddenly, you wouldn't mind that your family had to clean it up. Morbid, I know. Forgive me. But it's kind of a good thing to consider, too. No one wants to leave a mess behind for their grieving family to deal with.

Strategies for the cleanup

There are several methods you can use to organize your decluttering sessions, so in this section, I'll go through some of them so you'll be able to choose which will work best for you! But first, you should decide what kind of cleaner you are. Some of us, myself included, will be all-or-nothing kind of people. We want to get it all done as quickly as we can. If you're one of us, you might want to set aside a Saturday or even a whole weekend to devote to decluttering your entire house in one fell swoop. It can be incredibly tiring, but at the end of the day (or weekend), I find that it's also incredibly satisfying. Everything's done, and I can move on with my life and with making sure that it doesn't get so cluttered again! Doing it this way does have its challenges. First of all, setting aside the time to get it all done might be next to impossible if your family is very busy. Second, if you're not able to get it all done in the time you set aside, you might lose the momentum you had and never find the time or motivation to finish the job.

You might prefer to take a more slow-and-steady approach. You can tackle a small area every day or every few days until eventually, you have a decluttered house. Because each task only takes an hour or two, it'll be relatively easy to find the time. The challenge here, of course, is that your recently decluttered areas don't become re-cluttered before you're able to declutter the rest of the house. I also find that it's not quite as motivating. But that's just me.

Whatever type of cleaner you decide you are, one of these methods will likely be right up your alley.

The Minimalist Challenge

This method is great for those of you who aren't quite sure you want to jump all in. It starts you off at a slower pace, but as your momentum increases with each project completed, so does the pace. It makes getting started simple and relatively effortless.

It works like this: on the first day of a given month, choose one thing in your house to get rid of. On the second day, choose two things. On the third day, choose three things. And you get the point. It might sound agonizingly slow, but by the time the 30th day of the month rolls around, you will have gotten 496 items out of your house. That's no small number!

The trick with this challenge is to stay consistent. Don't miss a day because you'll end up behind and off schedule, which could make it hard for you to finish the challenge. Also, you don't have to start on the first day of the month, but it'll be easier to keep track of the days if you do. I wouldn't sacrifice the motivation you're feeling right now, though, in order to start at the beginning of a month, especially if you're only a week or so into a new month.

The Packing Party

This one sounds kind of fun to me, though I've never tried it, and it might sound absolutely crazy to you. However, it's a straightforward and low-risk way to get started because you actually won't be getting rid of anything right away. You do the decluttering first and worry about finding new homes for everything later. It also gives you a ton of free space instantly! Super cool.

The Packing Party is just what it sounds like: you start by packing up everything you own—except maybe the essential furniture like beds, your couch, and your dining room table and chairs. Label everything clearly so you would know what's in each box, and over the next few weeks, unpack only the things you need. As you go through the weeks, you'll find that you spend a lot less time going to your boxes because the things you use are already unpacked. Everything else is basically useless. Do this for about a month, then decide what you want to do with all of the things that are still in the boxes. Some of it might still be worth keeping, even if it stayed in the box for the entire month. For example, seasonal things like sports gear and Christmas lights could be kept, though you might want to minimize the amount of gear or lights you own. However, if you're able to leave most of the boxes unpacked, all the better! It'll be so much easier just to put the boxes in your car and drive them to a donation center!

The 12x12x12 Method

This method is great if you have an hour or two here or there to spend decluttering. It might not get your entire house decluttered very quickly, but if you spend a few hours doing this a couple of times a week, you'll chip away at all of the clutter until it's eventually clear.

During each cleaning session, you'll choose a total of thirty-six items in your house and sort them into three categories: things to put away, things to give away, and things to throw away.

In the "things to put away" category, you'll choose twelve items that you use on a regular basis. Once all thirty-six items are divided into their categories, these items have to be given a logical home. If you need to put it away because it's only used during a particular season, label the box clearly so it's easy to find later. Organize these items as you put them back, and when you get through every area of your house with this method, you'll not only have a decluttered house but an organized one as well.

The 4-(or-5)-Box Method

This method makes taking on one section of your house (a closet, a chest of drawers, etc.) quick and easy. All you do is get four or five boxes and label them: Give Away, Put Away/Keep, Throw Away, Not Sure, and (optionally) Sell. Then, set your boxes up next to whatever junk collector you plan to tackle and start going through each item. Quickly decide where each item belongs and toss it in the appropriate box. Rinse and repeat until the entire space is cleared, even of the items, you plan to keep. You'll replace those items later.

Once space is clear, choose a box and deal with it. It might be helpful for you to start with the easiest box to deal with first and move on to the harder ones as you go. Or, you might want to get the harder ones done and out of the way first. Whichever way works for you. You might also choose to simply put your Give Away box out of sight until you have several boxes and can make a trip to your local donation center. The same could be true of your Sell box. My only caution with putting these boxes away instead of dealing with them immediately is that you be careful not to forget to actually deal with them once you have a decent number of items to give away or sell. Otherwise, you're simply moving the clutter around. It's still good because it's out of the way and out of sight, but it's still there, so make sure to actually do something with all of it.

All of these strategies are great ways to get your momentum going and to make the decluttering process a little simpler. If none of these sounds useful to you, do some research to find a method that might work better. Or, simply do it your own way! However you choose to do it, just get in there and get it done!

CHAPTER 6
Important Places And Items

For me, one of the most important places to declutter is my bedroom because it's the place I go to relax on my own. When it's cluttered and messy, I can get extremely grumpy about it. And bless my husband's heart, he does not know how to put his own stuff away. So, I can be grumpy a lot.

I might be wrong for getting grumpy about it with my husband, but I'm not wrong in thinking that a decluttered bedroom is important. We've all known for pretty much as long as we've been around that sleep is not only important but necessary for life to be sustained. If we go without it for long, our very sanity starts to dissolve, and we could even die from exhaustion. Obviously, that's a bit dramatic for this discussion. The vast majority of us will never come close to being this exhausted. But if I have to go just a couple of nights without good rest, I can be extremely grumpy, and I struggle to think straight. I'm sure anyone reading this book has felt that kind of exhaustion.

Getting adequate rest is essential to maintaining the positive energy you'll need to make it through the decluttering process. By decluttering your bedroom first, you'll create a place of calm and relaxation in the midst of the chaos that'll help you get the rest you need. And declutter your own bedroom first! You might be tempted to do otherwise, but if you declutter your own bedroom first, you'll make sure you have the energy and motivation to help them declutter theirs. Not to mention, seeing you in your newly decluttered space is likely to make the transition smoother for your kids. They can see how clean and calm your room looks and how much you enjoy it, and it'll make it less scary for them to make the transition.

The first thing you need to consider when starting to declutter any space in your house is what the purpose of that space is. Go back to Chapter 2 and think about the purpose you've set out for your home and for each room inside. For many of us, our bedroom is where we relax and share alone time and intimacy with our partner. It may also serve as an office or a craft room. If that's the case, make sure that your secondary space is kept neat and decluttered as well and that there's some kind of visual barrier that helps divide the room. If at all possible, though, try to give your bedroom a single purpose.

Once you've determined the purpose you want your bedrooms to serve, you can set about getting rid of anything that doesn't serve that purpose. Should you have a TV in the bedroom? Probably not, since there have been many times I've found myself going to sleep way too late because I got caught up in a TV series, and I'm sure you've done the same thing. Should you keep the laundry basket right across from the bed? Not if it reminds you of all of the chores you still have to do. If your bedroom's purpose is to serve as a place of rest and connection with your partner, everything that distracts from that purpose has to go.

Then get started! Choose one of the methods we talked about in the last chapter and get to it. If you want to try the Packing Party, go to the store and grab some boxes, tape, and a marker (If you don't have these things already—don't add another Sharpie to your collection just because you can't think of where they might be! We're decluttering, here, not re-cluttering!). And get to packing. Put everything in a box except the absolute essentials, like your bed frame and the linens on your mattress. When you're done, put the date on the box, as well as a note about what's inside and put them to the side, preferably out of your bedroom, but somewhere you can see them every day. Enjoy your fully decluttered bedroom, and only unpack things you absolutely need. After a few weeks, revisit the boxes to see if there's anything in them that you missed, then decide what to do with the rest.

That method sounds particularly fun to me, but if you think that's just too much, pick another method! However, you choose to get it done, just make sure that you completely declutter the room so that you can enjoy a calm, relaxing oasis while you tackle the rest of the house!

Decluttering the Furniture

How many pieces of furniture do you have in your bedroom right now? Personally, my bedroom is tiny, and I have 7 pieces of furniture crammed in that space. Like I said, never beat yourself up too harshly if you come to a season where minimalism just isn't possible. I'm writing a book about minimalism, and even I have had to accept the season I'm in right now.

However, the more furniture you keep in your bedroom, the more surfaces there are to catch clutter. So, take as much furniture out as you can. If you have to keep a dresser in your room to store clothes, make sure you keep the top clear of clutter. But if at all possible, store all of your clothes in your closet or put your dresser inside the closet. It may not be this way now, but there was a time in my family's life when my husband and I had four simple pieces of furniture in our bedroom: a bed (obviously), two wall shelves, and a simple, clean-cut desk. A note about those wall shelves: The wall shelves actually serve as our bedside tables. Instead of keeping regular bedside tables there, with their extra clutter-accumulating shelves and drawers, we opted for a single surface on which to place only the essentials.

Decorations

Decorations are great. Believe me, I'm a decoration kind of girl! However, there's a balance between carefully placing just enough decorations to be tasteful and throwing so many decorations on your walls and surfaces that your room looks more cluttered. I know it's a hard concept to grasp, but white space is actually a good thing.

When deciding how many decorations to keep and where to put them, remember that less is more. Instead of covering a dresser or bookshelf with photos and trinkets, choose only one or two high-quality photos or decorations. Again, remember the purpose of your bedroom and choose your decorations accordingly.

Clothing and Linens

The thought of going through all of your clothes and linens might make you more stressed out and overwhelmed than the clutter itself. However, it can also be one of the most freeing parts of the whole decluttering process. Too many clothes only lead to continued decision fatigue (Chapter 4), so read this section, plan out how you want to do it, and get going. Trust me; you'll be glad you did.

- Quality over quantity
    - Owning a week's worth of the best clothes you can find (the ones that fit you best, that are made out of the best material, etc.) is so much better than owning a month's worth of mediocre clothes that don't fit you right and are cheaply made. It's ok to wear the same things from week to week. It's simpler, it's faster, and it's just plain easier than having to choose from a vast selection. Not to mention, if you only choose the clothes that look the absolute best on you, you'll always look amazing.
- Plan a capsule wardrobe
    - If you haven't heard of it before, a capsule wardrobe is an amazing thing for families who are trying to live minimalist lives. Essentially, it's a wardrobe that consists of only the…essentials, typically no more than 40 items total, including everything from winter to summer clothes, accessories, and pairs of shoes. The beauty of a capsule wardrobe is that each piece of clothing you own is high quality and is interchangeable with other pieces to create a variable wardrobe with only a few pieces. For example, a pair of jeans can be dressed up with a black blouse and a pair of black flats or dressed down with a t-shirt and a pair of tennis shoes. If you can fill your wardrobe with interchangeable pieces like this, your wardrobe will be small but efficient, which is exactly what it should be if you want a minimalist lifestyle!
- Be careful when you go shopping
    - We all know how tempting it is when you go shopping and you see a good sale. Before you go shopping, you should have a list already made out of what you need, just like you would for groceries. You should also have a good idea of what kinds of styles you like best and that work best for your lifestyle. That way, when you come across a great

sale, you can evaluate if you truly need the item or not. If you don't need it, don't get it! If you do, great! You've managed to save money while still only buying the things you need.
- Don't fall for all of the trends
  - Every season, the fashion industry churns out a few trendy items that are "in fashion" that particular season. And they're usually cute and great and make you feel like you fit in. But don't fall for it! Stick to your capsule wardrobe, full of high-quality pieces that work for you. Don't mess with it by trying to add all of the trendy items of the season. You'll end up right back where you started with a closet that's bursting at the seams.

Here's a couple of methods you could use to decide what clothes to keep and which ones should be given a new home:
1. The Last 2-Weeks
   - For this method, you'll take out everything you've worn in the last two weeks and pack up the rest. Over the next 30 days, use only the clothes you kept in the closet to see if you miss anything that had been packed away. If you didn't miss it, chunk it! Or, more responsibly, give it away.
2. The LUK Method
   - Every item in your wardrobe should adhere to the LUK rule: Do you like, use, and know each item? For example, if you have three pairs of jeans, but only one makes you feel amazing, just keep that one. If you have two pairs of tennis shoes but only use one for your daily exercise, just keep that one. And if you have five scarves but tend to forget that you even own three of them, keep only the two you remember. It's a simple method, but it gives you three easy-to-remember questions to ask of each item in your closet. If you don't like, use, or know it, toss it!

As far as linens go, I want you to first get it all out in one giant pile. Just plop it down in the living room floor and start sorting through it all, getting rid of any damaged linens or towels you come across. No one needs to keep all of those stained, hole-filled linens and towels in their home! Personally, I avoid using those like I avoid the plague, even though I know they're perfectly clean. There's just something nice about using a plush, soft, giant towel after a shower. Again, we're looking for quality over quantity, so only keep the linens and towels that are high quality (or that at least aren't just plain bad).

Once you've gotten rid of the dingy, stained, and hole-filled linens and towels, decide how many of each item you need to keep for your family. For most, having one towel per person, plus a few extra is enough. Hang the towels up after they've been used and use them for a couple of days. If something comes up and you're a day late doing laundry, start using the extra towels. Otherwise, one towel per person should be plenty. Sheets are kind of the same way, though you'll probably want an extra set of sheets for each bed, that way you don't have to get all of the sheets washed and dried before bedtime. So, keep two sets of sheets for each bed in your home. Pro tip: fold and store your sheets inside the matching pillowcase. That way, the entire set is stored together, and your linen closet is better organized.

Baby's Room

For the next little bit, we'll be going through each of the other bedrooms you could have in your home, namely, your kids' rooms. Each age group will have different needs, so we'll start with the easiest age group to declutter. It's the easiest because babies don't get much say in what goes in their rooms, nor do they actually care. Therefore, you get to make all of the decisions and don't have to fight a toy-hoarding 8-year-old every step of the way.

Furniture

Obviously, there are a few pieces of furniture that are essential to have in a baby's room, such as a crib. Some would say a diaper changing table and a comfortable chair are essential, though if money's tight, you can honestly do without both. You can't, however, do without a crib, and really, unless money is so tight you honestly can't buy the other two pieces, you'll be glad you invested in a changing table and a chair. However, other pieces of furniture like a full-sized dresser or bookshelf are completely unnecessary.

When you're deciding on a crib, try to think into the future. Do you plan to have more than one kid? If so, you could invest in a high-quality crib that will last through each of your future children's babyhood. Or you could get a crib that converts into a toddler bed if you plan only to have one child or want each of your kids to have a new crib. Either way, you plan to do it, do your homework on each potential crib to make sure it's safe and high-quality.

Gear

There are so many different kinds of baby gear out there! It's astonishing. As you start making these purchases, remember that your child will go through different stages. Purchase only the things that are necessary for each stage and donate everything they've grown out of as you go to avoid accumulating clutter. For example, a newborn doesn't need a high chair. Your baby won't really need one of those until he's ready to start eating baby food, so don't make that purchase before you really need to. Also, a toddler doesn't need a baby swing, so donate your old one! As I said, there's a lot of really cool gadgets out there that will claim to make your life easier. Don't fall into the trap! Purchase only the essentials for you and your lifestyle and forget about the rest!

Clothes

How often do you do laundry? Once a week, twice a week, every day? How often you choose to do laundry has a direct impact on how many outfits you need to have for your baby. Some minimalists recommend 3-4 outfits for a newborn, but let's be real: their newborns are either perfectly neat and never spit up, or they wash laundry at least every day, and who really has time for that? That's like being a prisoner to your laundry room! Personally, I try to wash laundry once a week, but it usually ends up being twice a week. If that's more your style too, you'll probably need at least 8 outfits, though it wouldn't be a bad idea to keep 10-14. That way, your baby has something clean to wear when he spits up all over his first outfit! Don't try to buy clothes for the future. Stick to the size your baby is currently wearing.

Books and Keepsakes

Babies and toddlers don't really need an entire library full of books. It may cause you to want to pull your hair out, but they generally like to listen to the same ones over and over again. So, keep a small library of about 8-15 books that your children really love.

As far as keepsakes go, start early by creating a space to store your baby's keepsakes, and add to it sparingly over the years. Maybe have one labeled box for each of your children's keepsakes. As they grow, you might have to add a box, but try to keep the number or keepsakes to a minimum.

Young child's room

Perhaps the most difficult age for decluttering comes during the toddler and preschooler phase, especially if they aren't already used to a minimalist lifestyle and have a lot of toys. If your preschooler is anything like mine, each of his toys is precious to him, even if he hasn't even looked at it in weeks. But try throwing it out, and he's on the floor in tears. Gracious.

However, it's also the time you can start teaching them why your family is choosing to live with less, and they can start helping you decide what belongs in their room and what can go. If you're able to get your toddler or preschooler on board, it can be fun to work with them.

As you start teaching your young child about minimalism, a few ground rules can be helpful:

- Everything needs to have a home. If you and your toddler or preschooler can't find a good home for it, it may not belong.
- Be generous. Young children might be selfish sometimes, but they can also be hugely generous and find great pleasure in giving to others. Teach your young child to be generous by helping her pick out toys to give to someone else and then taking her with you when you go to give them away.
- Family cleanup time is for everyone. Optimize your child's room so that it's easy for them to participate and help with family cleanup time. Make their toy storage easy for them to use (low to

the ground, simple, etc.) and teach them how to clean up their own belongings.

Older child's room

At this age, your child is likely ready for some more independence. Let them take responsibility for the cleanup by giving them some guidelines and let them have at it. Provide support and guidance as needed, but otherwise, let them take charge. Perhaps give them a specific space where they can put as many toys as they can reasonably fit and allow them to choose which toys go in the space and which ones have to find a new home. As far as their clothes go, allow them to take part in choosing what they want to wear. At this age, style might start to become important to them as they start going to school and wanting to fit in with their friends. Within reason, let them choose what clothes they want to keep in their wardrobe, but make it a simpler wardrobe with fewer items. Keeping about 10 outfits for each child is a pretty fair amount for the average family.

Teenager's room

If your persuading your preschooler to give up his toys was hard, convincing your teenager to give up some of their clothes could be just as difficult. Teenagers thrive on individuality and often place their identity in their clothing style and other material possessions they own. Before insisting that they have to declutter their entire space, talk with them about the advantages of a minimalist lifestyle in a way that will motivate them. For example, it will give them more time to spend with their friends or financial freedom to save up for a car. If you know there's a specific goal your teenager really wants, use it to help motivate him. If they're still hesitant, try to get them to declutter a single space in their room, like their closet or their desk. The key here is just to be patient and allow them to have as much independence with the process as possible.

CHAPTER 7
Furnitures And Other Items

As you move throughout your home, the next space you may want to consider decluttering is your living areas. These spaces are likely where your family goes to spend time together, and it's probably pretty cluttered, especially if you have young kids who like to keep their toys out. That would be my kid, by the way. It's great fun.

Anyway, before you get started going through your living spaces, get yourself set up. Choose the method that works best for you so far. If it's the four-box method, get four boxes out and label them. If it's the packing party, assemble several boxes and have a marker and tape ready to go. Decide where you might want to put the boxes or where you want to donate your giveaway box. Having all of this in mind before you even start will help make sure you actually get the job done instead of putting everything in boxes, only for them to remain where you left them for weeks.

So, get your boxes out, put on some comfy clothes, and let's get to work!

Furniture

Ah, the living room. A place to sit back, kick off your shoes, and binge-watch some Netflix after a long day. Or a place to sit down with your family, pull out a favorite board game, and go at it with some friendly competition. Whatever you and your family tend to do the most in your living room, it likely revolves around the furniture in the space. Everyone has their own spot on the couch. Do you play board games on the dining room table or on the coffee table? Do you have bookshelves filled with hundreds of books?

Whatever furniture you have in your living room, if it feels at all crowded or cluttered, it's probably too much. So, what pieces do you actually need in your living spaces and which ones could probably be moved or even disposed of?

To make these decisions, you have to consider your space. How big is it? What is its shape? Where are the doorways and windows? You also have to think about the room's purpose. Go back to chapter 2 and look at the purpose you laid out for your living spaces. What pieces fit with that purpose and which ones aren't entirely necessary? How many seats do you really need at the dinner table? Enough to fit a small army? Probably not. Enough to fit your family and maybe a couple of guests? That's more like it.

As you go throughout the room, ask yourself questions about each piece of furniture that's already in the room: is it necessary? Does anyone actually use it? Could a smaller piece serve the same purpose as a larger one? Does it look right/fit well in the space?

Bookshelves

I love books. I'm a reader and a writer, and I just love them. I own hundreds of books. But I only have a single shelf for my books. Strange? Impossible? Not really. I went digital. My husband and I both have Kindles, where 95% of our books are stored. Only the really important ones are kept in paperback. Hence, only one shelf for hundreds of books. It's great.

In the past, bookshelves have been a necessity to store books, CDs, DVDs, etc. However, with the advent of the digital age, we now have the option of storing such items on computers and tiny little boxes that attach to our televisions like Apple TV, Fire TV, Roku, etc. Kindles, Nooks, and Kobo e-readers can hold hundreds upon hundreds of books on a device that easily fits in the palm of your hand. Movies can be stored and watched on apps such as VUDU and iTunes Movies. Walls lined with bookshelves have become a thing of the past, so take advantage of it! Start building your digital libraries instead of continuing to hold onto your physical ones and get rid of those shelves!

Decorations

Here's a new concept for many of us: not every space has to be filled! In fact, there's something relaxing about white space. It looks clean, fresh, and calm. As you go through your living spaces, I'd actually recommend that you start your new minimalist lifestyle without any decorations at all. Give yourself time to feel and enjoy the empty spaces and clear surfaces. Then you can add a few pieces here and there that really add beauty to the room, instead of just adding clutter.

Coffee Tables

Do you really use your coffee table to hold a cup of coffee? Better yet, does a cup of coffee need a space as large as a coffee table? If your answer to these questions is no, you will probably do well to find a smaller solution to your drink-holding needs. A small end table between two chairs or at the end of the couch could serve you well.

Electronics

I believe I told you about my husband's obsession with electronics? It's especially bad with the TV in the living room. There are wires going everywhere; he's always taking cords or the Apple TV and moving them to another part of the house. It drives me batty.

Besides driving me batty, the television situation also contributes to a lot of our family's struggles. Our young son has gotten addicted to watching TV, something we woefully regret allowing to happen. My husband and I get into fights over where the HDMI cord is to the Apple TV or why he spends so much time trying to put all of our movies on this server thing (Sorry, I'm not an expert in electronics, you guys.). I find myself binging far too often on Netflix shows. I try to tell myself it's just for the noise. Except then I get sucked into the show, and all of my productivity goes out the door! It's a problem.

If you're anything like my family, you probably have many of the same issues. Your husband or wife may not spend too much time putting movies on a server, but it could be watching sports instead of playing with the kids, binging on a favorite show instead of getting the laundry done. Whatever issues your family faces when it comes to electronics, it could be easily fixed by simply getting rid of it. Believe it or not, television is not a necessity. It's hard for me to believe it too sometimes. But it's not.

If you're really dedicated to this idea of minimalism and to spending more time with your family, I highly recommend getting rid of the TV. Whether you chuck it out altogether or put it away for a time, having no TV can be incredibly beneficial to everyone in the household.

Even if you decide that going radical and chunking out the TV isn't for you and your family, you could likely pare down your electronics quite a bit. Does everyone in the house need an iPhone, an iPad, and Kindle? Probably not. Limit your kids to one device each (depending on their age). Designate an area in the living space as a charging station, where devices should be kept unless they're being used. Place time limits on device usage and hold to them strictly. No child needs to be glued to a device for hours upon end. As a mom dealing with this with my own kid, believe me, you want to set limits!

Sentimental items

It can be really, really difficult to say goodbye to an item that holds sentimental value. They hold fond memories for us and make us feel safe and comforted. They help us remember family members and loved ones who have passed away and left something special for us to keep. Many times, getting rid of such items can feel a bit like chopping your own hand off: painful, unnecessary, and just plain horrible. However, there are a few things you should keep in mind:

The value isn't in the item itself. It's in the memories and character of the person the item reminds you of. You don't need a specific item in order to honor and remember a loved one. That person is forever in your heart and mind.

Life isn't about living in the past. It's about being present in the moment and looking toward the future. Holding onto sentimental items that only add to the clutter and disorganization of your home means that you're holding onto the past too tightly. It's good to remember what has happened and the people you've loved in the past, but it's unhealthy to hold on too tightly.

You could take photos of sentimental items and keep them in a photo book. If you don't need the item, you just don't need it. That doesn't mean you want to forget about it, though. Hold onto it by taking a photo of it instead of keeping it in your house to add to the clutter.

Keep a single box for really important things. Sometimes you just can't let go of something, and that's ok. Either find a truly useful way to use it in your home or put it in a single box where you house all of your keepsakes that are too important to lose. Just be very selective about what goes in the box and keep it to a minimum.

Special spaces for the kids

In many homes, toys kid's belongings tend to start trickling out into areas they don't belong. My three-year-old has toys in every conceivable corner of our house. As you start decluttering your house and reorganizing it for maximum efficiency, you may consider setting aside a specific area of your home for your kids' toys and activities. I'm as big a fan of independent play as any busy mom, and it can be useful to have a stimulating, fun area for your children to play in that doesn't creep out into the entire home.

If you decide you want to create a space for your children to play, be sure to consider the design of the area carefully. Instead of going at it with all kinds of closed-ended toys, invest in good, educational, and open-ended social options like dolls, crayons, play dough, and puzzles. A chalkboard wall is a great option, especially for younger kids. It gives them a chance to write on the wall with immunity, and what child doesn't want to do that?

You should choose items that promote sharing and teamwork. Encourage your kids to share with each other and work together to solve puzzles or play games.

You should choose items that promote creativity. Create an art table, where all of their art supplies (at least the ones that can't really cause a lot of damage if left unsupervised) are easily accessible. Keep only a few toys in the space, so they have to be creative and innovative with their play.

Finally, as with any area of your home, you should consider your purpose for the area and for your kids. Is it for them to be independent, creative, and willing to share? Then your space should reflect that purpose, and everything that goes into it should do the same.

A special note here: if one of your goals is for your children to be independent and responsible, make sure that everything in the space is both accessible to them and safe for them to use without constant supervision. If you have young children, this space might be in the living room, where they can still be supervised while playing independently. However, if you have older kids, they might appreciate a little more privacy and independence, so set up their space in their bedroom if you feel comfortable.

Again, however, you choose to do this, it's important for children to have space for their imagination and independence to grow along with them—without infringing upon everyone else's space and your sanity!

CHAPTER 8
Confessions And Steps

Quick confession: I hate cooking. Well, hate might be a strong word. It's more like I hate planning meals for the week and grocery shopping, both of which have to happen in order to cook. Once both of those things have happened and I have everything neatly laid out and ready to go, I actually enjoy cooking, especially when I'm alone in the kitchen with a glass of wine and my favorite TV show playing on my iPad. But let's be real: I have a three-year-old and a newborn. That never happens.

Instead, there's usually a little boy clinging to my leg or opening all of the cabinets behind me. Or a baby is crying because he dropped his pacifier. Or a husband is trying to tell me something about his day. It's often loud and chaotic and not exactly relaxing.

But it's also a great place for my family to hang out and spend time together. As long as the dangerous items are out of reach, it's a relatively safe place for my three-year-old to play while I'm watching. He likes to "help" me cook, which usually only makes a huge mess but is super cute and sweet. My husband likes to sit at the table while I cook, talking to me about something interesting that happened that day or working on a project he has going. So as hectic and crazy as it can get, I do enjoy the kitchen, even if I don't often get to cook in my perfect set of conditions.

I imagine that your kitchen is probably very similar. Lots of people refer to their kitchen as the heart of their home. It's often where the kids work on their homework, where families sit down to eat a meal together, and where the delicious smell is constantly inviting everyone in the home to come to enjoy the fun. It can also be an extremely stressful place, as papers pile up on the counter, the trash can starts to smell because your son forgot to take it out last night, and appetizers for the part you're hosting start burning on the stove.

You may not always be able to control how many people follow you into the kitchen (nor would you really want to). You might not always get the recipe just right or have a perfectly clean trash can. Try as you might, you just can't control other people, and sometimes your child will forget to take the trash out. However, you can control what items belong in your kitchen and where they are placed. Decluttering your kitchen could be just the solution you need to make one of your most hectic, memory-filled spaces a calm and relaxing place.

First Steps

As always, when you first get started decluttering a new space, remind yourself why you're doing this in the first place. Why do you want your home and your lifestyle to be minimalistic and simple? What is the purpose of your kitchen? After you've reminded yourself why you want to do this, it'll be so much easier to find the motivation to push through the hard work.

Next, it'll be easier to declutter your kitchen if it's clean and everything is put away. So, make sure it's in its normal, clean state (not it's normal, dirty state, mind you!). All of the dishes are clean and put away in their proper place. All of the counters are clear of papers, food, and any other items that don't belong in the kitchen. The stove, sink, and counters are wiped down, and the floors are swept and mopped.

Decide how quickly you want this done. Do you have a day to tackle it all at once? Or do you have an hour here and there to declutter one or two cabinets at a time? Whatever choice you make, just make sure that you have enough time to get it all done! There's nothing worse than pulling everything out of a cabinet and not having enough time to put what you decide to keep back.

Personally, I think it's easiest to try to do the kitchen all at once. I'm generally more apt to do things that way anyway, but with the kitchen, I think it's especially useful. If it's been a while since you've decluttered and reorganized your kitchen, you likely have similar items in different places. You might also want to move items to a different area of the kitchen. The problem with tackling one spot at a time is that if you do want to rearrange, there's not much room to do it because everywhere else in the kitchen is still filled. That's just my personal opinion, though. Feel free to do it however you want! As long as it happens, that's all that matters.

In your kitchen-decluttering adventures, try to replace items where you might actually use them. For example, keep your oven mitts close to the oven. Place your dishwashing soap under the sink, next to the dishwasher. And put your pots and pans near the stove. Just do what makes sense for you and the way you use your kitchen.

Cabinets and drawers

Now that you have your kitchen ready to go, you can get down to the real business at hand: decluttering and reorganizing your kitchen for maximum efficiency and minimum clutter. You can start at any point in the kitchen, so let's start with the cabinets and drawers. Getting started with this part of the kitchen is great, especially if you only have a few minutes at a time for the decluttering process. You can work on one cabinet or drawer at a time, getting rid of anything that isn't used often or is sometimes forgotten about. You could also choose a category that might belong inside that particular cabinet. For example, if you choose to start with the cabinet next to your stove, you could gather all of the pots and pans throughout the kitchen and arranging them neatly inside that cabinet.

This method is called decluttering by category, and it is incredibly useful for taking note of all of your duplicates. If you have multiple copies of similar items, it is easy to get rid of all but one of them. For example, if you have two or three mixing bowls of the same size, chunk two of them, and keep just one.

As you go through each cabinet and drawer, you might as well take the time to wipe down each of them to make sure they're clean. After all, it's not often that you have a chance to get those cabinet shelves clean!

As with all of the space in the house, you will need to ask yourself questions about each item you consider getting rid of. Do you use the item very often? Do you own something else that could serve the very same purpose? Do you like it? Does it still work well? Again, every item in your kitchen should follow the LUK guidelines: you should like, use, and/or know each and every item you own.

There are so many items that a lot of people keep in their kitchens that are very rarely used, especially in the small appliance department. Things like ice cream makers, sandwich grills, bread machines, rice cookers, air fryers, all of them tend to be quickly bought but rarely used. If you happen to be someone who uses one of these small appliances often, keep it! However, if you're like the rest of us and you find that you are pulling these small appliances out from the back corners of your cabinets, you probably aren't using them very often, and they can be thrown in the give-away pile.

Get those counters clear!

Ok, I don't know if you've noticed this in your own home, but the horizontal surfaces in my home are not my friend. I get lulled into thinking they're my friend, but then inevitably, they turn on me. They become the greatest ally to my hoarding tendencies because they hold things so nicely! Also, it's super easy to simply plop your stuff down on the counter and walk away from it. My horizontal spaces are a mess!

In your kitchen, you're definitely going to want to clear off your countertops. So here are some tips that might help you clear your kitchen counters off for good!

First of all, set up a command center somewhere in your home. It doesn't have to be in your kitchen, but if you find that it's where your family tends to dump all of their homework, papers, backpacks, and everything else they own, the kitchen might be a natural place for your command center. That's where my family's belongings generally end up, so that's why I'm bringing up the command center here.

A command center is really whatever you need it to be. It can simply be a place for your family members to place their papers without causing the counters to become cluttered. It could include a family calendar and a list of chores or anything else you think might be useful for everyone in your family to see and have access to on a daily basis. It can (and definitely should) contain a basket for small items like keys or wallets that are usually just dumped anywhere and easily lost.

One thing I would recommend is that, whatever you choose to include in your family's command center, you set it up inside a cabinet, probably a top cabinet if all of the children you want to have access to it are tall enough to reach it (after all, you wouldn't want your toddler to reach in and pull everyone's papers out every day). Your countertops are going to be a clutter-free zone, so don't even start inviting more clutter. Even organized clutter can drive you crazy. Have your small-item basket in the cabinet as well as a paper organizer with each slot labeled with a different family members' name. That slot then becomes the place where that person can dump any papers they have. If you want to have a family calendar or chore chart, attach it to the back of the cabinet door so that it's out of sight but still easily accessible.

Once you have set up a command center in your kitchen that will be natural and easy for your family to use, you can start enforcing a clutter-free zone on the kitchen counters. From this point forward, nothing goes on the counters that do not belong there. Here's a radical idea for you: you might even decide that all of the small appliances that usually live on your counters can be put away. I know, I know. Crazy, right? You should definitely give it a try, though. Having completely clear counters might sound ludicrous, but it is actually incredibly freeing and is a great sight to walk into. I completely get that you might not want to have to get your toaster oven or coffee maker out of the cabinet every morning, but you might also find that you enjoy the feeling of clear counters more than the convenience of having them there all the time. So, I encourage you to give it a try. Put your coffee maker in the cabinet directly above its normal spot, that way it's easy to pull out and put back up. It really doesn't take that much longer, and I think you will find you like it.

What to do with the cookbooks?

Ok, now that you have cleared off all of your countertops and gotten rid of all of your duplicate gadgets and tools that you thought were oh-so-necessary, it's time to go through those cookbooks you've held onto for ages. Let's be honest: most of us don't use cookbooks anymore. We might hold onto them for sentimental value, but we generally don't use them very often. Most of our recipes are found online today. We save them on apps that are extremely useful. There are plenty of really great ones that you can save your favorite recipes too. You can even keep an inventory of the items in your pantry so that you can easily search for recipes that you have the ingredients for. It's great for meal planning. I definitely encourage you to look some up and try them out.

That being said, cookbooks aren't that necessary anymore, but I get it. Your precious great-grandmother used to use this one cookbook for ages and ages. It's been worn by years of helping prepare delicious and nutritious meals for generations of your family members, and now it's been passed down to you, and you feel horrible for throwing it out. That's fine. Treat it like a sentimental item. Keep it and store it where you store your sentimental items. That's fine.

However, we all have cookbooks that hold absolutely no sentimental value. They might have a recipe or two that we like, but they aren't used daily or even weekly. Or usually even monthly. Most of the time not even quarterly. Again, those apps that I was talking about earlier are great for these things. You can find the recipes you like in these books and type them into the app. It takes a minute, but once you've done it, it's there. The ingredients will be compiled, and you can search for them based on what you have in your pantry. And then you can get rid of the cookbook. It's pretty darn great.

If you decide that you have to keep a cookbook, set some guidelines for yourself. Make sure that there are at least five recipes that you all the time in the cookbook. I would still recommend uploading the recipe into an app on your phone, simply because of the clutter cookbooks contribute and how useful those apps can be.

Or, if you are not super keen on the idea of using an app for your recipes, you can also create your own binder where you write down the recipe, type it out and print it off, tear out the page (probably don't do this one!), however you choose to do it. Get a binder and some tabbed dividers. Write the different categories of food on the tabs, and you're on your way to having one single binder for all of your recipes.

I know it might be tough, but getting rid of the cookbooks will free up a lot of space in your kitchen.

CHAPTER 9
Decorations And Decluttering

I know I've said this about a hundred times, or at least it seems like it, but one great place to start your decluttering journey is actually the bathroom, especially if you are hesitant or nervous about minimalism or if you simply don't have the time to get started on a bigger project. The bathroom is great because it's usually a very small room, and you generally don't store sentimental items there. The hardest decision you'll probably have to make is which color lipstick to toss out and which ones actually look good enough on you for you to keep.

For many of us, especially those of us who are women, our bathrooms are filled with all of the beauty products, skin care products, age-defying products, and anything else you can think of. Our medicine cabinets are full to bursting. Believe me, the bathroom is full of things that will be painless to get rid of, so I recommend that you just start chunking. What makes it even easier is that no one wants half-used shampoo, so there's generally no use in trying to gather everything up to give away to someone. Now, if it is completely unopened and you feel led to, I know there are certain places that could use some of the more generic bathroom products like shampoo and conditioner and body wash, and maybe even some makeup. However, most of the things you find in your bathroom, you'll simply want to throw away.

So, get started! Go through your drawers and your cabinets and pull out anything and everything you don't use every day. As far as your makeup goes, take an incredibly critical look at everything in your makeup bag, drawer, or whatever, and decide if it's something you really use and need or if it's something that's in there but you rarely use it or you don't really need it. Cut your makeup to the bare minimum and put away the rest.

If you're feeling nervous about doing this, you might put it in a box, label it, set it in the garage, and live with what you have in your bathroom for a few days, a week, maybe even a few weeks to see if you really even miss what you put away. I'm willing to bet that you won't. Most of the time, when we have a surplus of items in our bathroom, it's because we're searching for that perfect thing to make our eyelashes longer or our hair less frizzy. But we usually end up going back to the same things over and over again.

So, unless your skin is genuinely abnormally dry or your hair is very curly and frizzy, you probably don't need a wide variety of specialty products for every member of your family. Generic, multipurpose products work just fine. I even bought the cheapest shampoo and conditioner I could possibly find the other day, and my family's hair is still clean and soft. I haven't even noticed a difference.

Decluttering

Decluttering your bathroom is really an easy thing to do. All you have to do is start pulling things out and tossing anything you haven't used in the last week. Or, if you're feeling a little bit more ready for your bathroom to be cleared, you can even get rid of everything you haven't touched in the last day or two. That's getting bold right there. Or, you could do this method, but then keep the few items you use once a week or every other week for special occasions. You can store these items in a separate container that belongs under the sink or somewhere that isn't as easily accessible as all of your everyday items. Once you've decided what those everyday essentials are, return them to a place in your bathroom that is out of sight, and/or natural to access.

If you don't have enough storage in your bathroom, you can try to add storage by hanging a cabinet or a few shelves on the wall. But as with the kitchen, you should try your best to keep all horizontal surfaces clear. Your bathroom will be much calmer and more relaxing, and you'll thank yourself for it later when you aren't using your precious, alone, bath time to put away all of the clutter on the countertops. As far as the rest of your products go, you can either toss it out wholesale, or you can gather some of the less-used items and donate them to a local donation center or shelter. They may not want half-used specialty beauty products, but I'm sure they could certainly use shampoo, conditioner, and body wash, as well as some of your gently used grooming products like hair brushes and nail clippers.

A note about medicine: I don't know why people tend to store their medicine in a damp area like the bathroom. It doesn't make any sense to me. Although to be completely honest, I totally did this for the longest time. However, if you do keep your medicine in the bathroom you might find that the kitchen is a more natural place to store the medicine, just don't store it right next to the stove or the oven. So, consider moving your medicine to the kitchen, as long as you know that it's accessible to those who need it and not accessible to those who shouldn't be able to use it, as your toddler. Also be sure to check the expiration dates on your medicines because it's very easy to lose track of, and if you're anything like me, you have a lot of expired medications in your medicine cabinet. Just make sure you follow any guidelines your community might have for getting rid of old medication.

Decorations

Again, I'm a decoration kind of girl. I like to have a vase with a single, simple flower in it or a picture frame or some other kind of decoration to brighten up a room and make it feel like home. It's perfectly fine if you're the same way. However, the bathroom is usually a small space, and adding much extra to that space will immediately make it feel cluttered.

So, either do without decorations at all, or if you find that to be boring or un-homey, place one small decoration, perhaps two, and leave it be. In a small space like the bathroom, less is generally more.

Adding in your kids

Depending on the bathroom situation in your home, you may share a bathroom with your kids, or you may (blessedly) have your own bathroom while your children have their own. Whatever the situation is, getting rid of all of the clutter in their bathroom will greatly help them be able to use the bathroom without having things to distract them. They'll be able to use the bathroom without getting into the bathtub toys every time, and they'll also be able to clean the bathroom on their own, depending on their age.

If you have teenagers, the decluttering process might be a little more complicated, especially if your teenager is a female. If that's the case, and your teenager is not fully on board with the minimization process, you might allow them a bit of independence on this. Set some guidelines that you're comfortable with, show them what your bathroom looks like, and then let them decide how they want to follow the guidelines you've set in place. For all of your kids, no matter their ages, minimalism is partly about teaching them the difference between needs and essentials versus extras, clutter, and wants. But for your teens, this is especially true because they'll be on their own in a few short years, and they'll need to be able to make these decisions on their own. So, let them have the freedom and independence to go through this process on their own, only helping them out if they need it.

Again, the bathroom is a pretty easy place to declutter, so don't overthink it. Just throw anything you don't use every day in a box, donate it, chunk it, throw it in the trash. That's really all there is to it.

CHAPTER 10
Aspects To Embrace

If you're lucky enough to have a separate room for your office, consider yourself blessed. Personally, I do not have an office, and I'm sitting in my kitchen, trying to write this book for you. It's going super well. But I would love an office with a door. However, having a home office can also serve as a repository for extra clutter. It's an entire room that you don't really need a whole lot of space in because sitting at a desk with a computer doesn't take up an entire room. Therefore, the entire room fills up with your extra clutter. If you have a large desk, those pesky horizontal spaces will fill up with paper, pens, post-it notes, and anything else that can fit on it.

Again, I truly believe you are blessed if you have one of these rooms, and I certainly would love one. However, it can be a tricky room to control because it's often viewed as an extra room simply for clutter. There might be a desk with a computer and a chair. But the rest is for clutter. So, in order to reclaim your beautiful home office space that many of us would die for, the first thing you should do is just take out anything and everything that doesn't help you get your work done. Take out anything that doesn't relate to your work. Sort everything on your desk. Go through all of the papers and decide whether they should be shredded or kept.

Once you've done the initial cleaning of the room to get rid of the clutter, you can get started preparing your office for continued minimalism and productivity.

What do you really need in an office?

As always, the first thing you need to do after you have cleaned the room is to consider the purpose of your office. What do you do there? Is it strictly for your work and no one else'? Do your kids have their own desk on which they do homework? Do you meet with clients in your home office? Whatever you do in your office, pick out the furniture and other items that are absolutely essential to that purpose, and nothing else.

Furniture

If you work online, and most of your work is done only on the computer, it's likely that you'll only need a small desk and a computer chair. However, if you meet with clients, you might decide that you want an entire living space in your office so that you can consult with your clients in a comfortable, calming environment. Or, if your kids study there alongside you, you might have an extra desk or two that your kid's study on, along with a corresponding computer chair. Of course, along with more desks come the pesky horizontal spaces so you might want to be careful about how much horizontal space you keep in the area.

Electronics

What electronics do you really need in your home office? Do you really need a separate scanner? Have you even used the fax machine behind you since 1998? If the answer to either of those questions is no, pack them up and move 'em out. It's likely that you'll need a printer. Regardless of how much I like working digitally, it can still be useful to have a pen and paper to scratch out ideas, and sometimes it's even necessary for signing papers and returning them.

A great option is that many printers these days come with a scanner attached, which allows you to have both a printer and a scanner without taking up the space that both devices would have used in the past.

Office supplies

Office supplies! We love them! We love to collect them. We love to hoard them. However, most of them are never used, especially if most of your work is done online. So, chuck it. You only need one stapler, one pair of scissors, a small handful of pens and pencils, and maybe a highlighter or two. Depending on your work, you might need a few more specialized items. However, the point here is that you get rid of anything that is unnecessary or that is duplicated. If you already have it, don't keep it. Chunk it. It's easy to accumulate extras over the years.

Mail

Mail is awful. It's either junk mail or it's a bill. I never get good mail anymore. It's sad. However, you might not just want to throw it all away because some of it might actually be important. So, go through whatever mail you have and chunk all of the junk (hey, that rhymes!) and sort through everything else to see if you need to keep it. If you do find something that you need to keep, put it in an organizer that is clearly labeled with the categories of paperwork you might have, such as bills, bank statements, etc.

There are ways to control the amount of mail you get. Most bills can be paid online these days, and it's really very easy to switch from paper billing to electronic. In fact, most companies would prefer you pay electronically. Not only does it reduce paper waste, but it also saves both you and the company time, money, and effort writing the check, paying for postage, and delivering it to the post office. In addition, most banking needs can be met online. It's definitely something to look into, so I highly recommend it. It will help you immensely in minimizing the amount of mail you get.

Papers

If there's anything I hate more than mail, it's papers! Or at least, I hate it just as much as mail because it's basically the same thing since most of my paper comes from my mail. It's so easy for the paper to become cluttered and disorganized because we tend to get in the habit of just stuffing paper anywhere that has space. We rarely take the time to develop the habit of putting the paper where it belongs. Personally, I'm rather good at creating organization systems at the start, but it never fails that I'll come across a piece of paper that doesn't fit in my organization system, so I stuff it anywhere I can, and from there, the disorganization erupts.

However, the only way to truly master the paper clutter is to simply be disciplined about your organization system. Create it from the start, keep a handful of empty folders available at all times so it's easy to create a new folder when a need arises. Every category of paper that you keep should have a home, so receipts, insurance papers, bills, tax returns, etc. all need to have a separate folder or binder. If at all possible, always put your papers away immediately. As soon as one appears on your desk, find its home. Don't let it linger on your desk.

Personally, I try to keep as little paper as possible. I digitize most of my papers because it's very easy for me to lose physical paper. Like with paper files, I'm fairly good at creating an organization system, but not very good at maintaining it. However, unlike paper files, with digital files, if I look hard enough, I will be able to find it. Paper files are usually just lost. I do need to get better about maintaining organization, though. I would try to choose one or the other: physical or digital. If you try to keep both, you'll end up paying a lot more because you'll be paying for the digital storage service, as well as the supplies to keep or physical files organized. So, choose one, organize it effectively, and be disciplined about sticking with it.

Embrace the digital age

This time period in the life of the world is extremely cool. What used to require stacks and stacks of paper and hours and hours of library research is now done on a single screen with a laptop that weighs less than a bag of sugar and takes only a quick Google search that leads me to all of the resources I could ever need. As I said, it's pretty cool.

I know that a lot of people are a little bit hesitant to completely embrace the digital age, though. It's a little unfamiliar, and a lot of people aren't confident enough in their digital skills, so they choose to remain analog for a lot of their needs. However, if you simply take the time to learn how to do it in the first place, I promise that digitizing your life will make it simpler and much more space-friendly.

Scan old photos that are currently collecting dust in a box in a corner and be excited that you will never lose those photos. Get rid of all of those DVDs and CDs that have been taking up space in your office for ages. Get an Apple Music subscription where you can listen to and even download all of the music you could possibly want. Pay for Netflix or Hulu every month or one of the other great TV streaming services, and I promise you won't miss your giant DVD collection for long. You can even buy digital movies online and build up a movie collection that way. You can also buy a Kindle. They're amazing for storing hundreds upon hundreds of books on a tiny little device instead of lugging around stacks of books that are heavy and take up a lot of space.

Set up your bills so that you receive statements electronically. Choose electronic magazine subscriptions instead of paper ones so that you can get rid of the clutter they create on your desk. Take a picture of the cover of any device manuals you think you might need. As long as you have the model number, I promise you can find the full manual online.

Like I said before, the advances of the digital age are incredibly useful and can make your life so much easier. It might take some time to learn, but I think that you'll find it's worth. Be careful with your digital space, though.

As cool as going digital can be, you also don't want to just throw all of your physical clutter into the computer and create a mess for yourself there. Digital clutter can be just as frustrating as physical clutter. So, start this process right by first creating an organization system for yourself and then starting to add your photos, papers, movies, etc. Whatever storage option you choose (Dropbox, iCloud, etc.) create a home for everything you might put in there and schedule time every week to make sure that it's organized and maintained.

Personally, I like to keep the desktop of my laptop completely clear. It's kind of like a horizontal space in my house. It's the place my eyes immediately go to when I open up my computer, and it's much happier for me if I open it up, see a cute picture of my kids and nothing else. If there are a ton of files cluttering the screen, it stresses me out and that's not good. So, I recommend that you try to keep your desktop as clear as any other horizontal space in your home. If you have to have a folder on your desktop (because it is very convenient), create just one folder to dump everything in that you might need it for and then at the end of the day, go back through that folder and put everything in its proper place.

I don't know about you, but I love that my smartphone has a camera. It's a great camera, too, and it's specifically why I bought the phone. However, it makes it extremely easy to simply start tapping that little white button to take dozens of pictures at one single time, so I have a lot of pictures that are very similar. If you have young kids, it can be incredibly useful because their facial expressions change on a moment-by-moment basis. You might get a really horrible, sad picture one second and a really precious and cute picture the next. You just never know what you're going to get, so being able to take multiple pictures is a great thing. However, it also takes up storage space on my phone or on my computer, so it's important that you regularly go through your photos and clear out the ones that you don't need. Pick out a few of your favorites from those dozens-long duplicate sessions and delete the rest.

Also, be sure that you back everything up. Computers are great. They work great most of the time. But there are times that they crash.

Sometimes digital storage options fail, and you could risk losing your digital photos and paperwork. I highly recommend that you not only purchase an online digital storage solution like Dropbox or iCloud but that you also buy a physical hard drive so that your digital files are always backed up on a physical device.

Another area of the digital world that is notorious being cluttered is email. I don't know about you, but I personally have a ton of junk email. Some of it is stuff that I actually enjoy reading and want to be kept up to date one, but a lot of it is useless and just takes up space in my inbox. So, depending on how quickly your email gets cluttered, you should definitely set aside time on a regular basis to go through your emails and decide which ones you want to keep and which ones you can delete.

The digital world is definitely a great one, and it's worth learning how to put your physical paper files into a digital file for a lot of reasons. However, you should always be careful to keep your digital space decluttered, just as you would your physical space.

CHAPTER 11
Humanity

Ok, so far, we've talked about what minimalism is, how to develop a mindset of minimalism that will appeal to your entire family. We've discussed guidelines that you might want to set for your family, as far as what goes into your house, what your home's purpose is, and how to treat the items that remain in your house. We've talked about strategies for decluttering your home, including the 4-box method, the packing party and the 12x12x12 method. We've talked about specific tips for decluttering your bedrooms, your living spaces, your kitchen, your bathroom, and your office. And by this point, I hope that you have gained a greater appreciation for the benefits of minimalism. However, unless you're completely naive, I'm sure you're aware that this process might not be an easy one for everyone in your family. Some people simply like their stuff, and they don't want to be told that they need to get rid of it. Regardless of who is presenting the resistance, I promise you it will come, and it won't be fun. However, I hope to provide you with some tips for dealing with the resistance that will help you navigate it without causing more conflict or stress in your family's life.

The Beauty of Humanity

The beauty of humanity is that every single one of us is completely unique and different. We have our own hobbies, our own interests, our own wants and desires, dreams, and needs. And it's a beautiful thing. It's what makes the world such a diverse and interesting place to live in. However, it can also be a little bit frustrating. If I were, to be honest like I've tried to be throughout this book, my husband and I have very different opinions on what decluttering means. I might want to wholesale chunk out everything we own except for the major things like my computer, our furniture, and a few sentimental items. He, on the other hand, will want to keep about 60% of the stuff that we own. He'll want to keep the duplicated can openers because one works differently than the other. He has a stack of journals that he doesn't want to get rid of, even though most of them aren't even filled. We're different that way, and it can be frustrating. In the past, when we have worked on decluttering our home, we both generally agree that it's something that needs to be done and that we should get started doing it as soon as possible. We agree with the purpose we have for our family. We agree on the purpose of each room in our house. But for whatever reason, we don't tend to agree on how it should be done. He's more of a slow-and-steady person, and I'm more of a get-it-done kind of person. Now, to give him credit, he is much better at maintaining a decluttered house than I am. I tend to purge it all, get it out, be done, and then allow clutter to start trickling back into the house rather quickly. He, on the other hand, is much better about resisting the new forms of clutter. So, the point is, we're all different. We all frustrate each other, and it's just something you're going to have to deal with. Through this chapter, I hope that you can find some strategies that will help you to do that.

Find your people

Before you really start confronting your resistant family members, I would recommend finding people who are already on the same page as you. It can be incredibly helpful and relieving to find other people who think the same way as you do. They can often help you decide how to approach your less-than-enthusiastic family members, and they'll be people you can go to when you feel frustrated, defeated, and a little bit crazy. So, I definitely encourage you to join a Facebook group or find people in your community who are already on the minimalism journey because you'll find that they are a great source of ideas and encouragement. If your family members can't be that for you in this particular area of life. However, I would caution that you don't use the Facebook group or your friendships as a place to harp on the negatives and the frustrations your family might bring. The other people in your home have a right to their own thoughts and opinions on things and you shouldn't use your platforms to bash them for disagreeing with you, no matter how frustrated you might become at times. So, ask for encouragement, ask for support, vent a little bit about your frustrations if you have to, but always come back to something positive about your family members because they deserve your respect, whether you agree with them or not.

Remind them of the benefits

Personally, my idea for simplifying our home is specifically for my family to have a better life. In our highly cluttered and busy home, it's difficult to feel connected with any of them truly. I'm constantly cleaning or being frustrated that I just cleaned and it's already dirty again or telling my kids to go clean their rooms or being frustrated with my husband that he has left dirty laundry on the floor. Simplicity is for my family. I want to be able to connect with them better, and I believe that owning fewer things will help us to do that. For your kids, I would recommend just kind of constantly bringing it up in everyday conversation. Slide in a comment every once in a while, about how great it is that there's not too much stuff to clean up because it means you'll be able to get to the park earlier or spend more time at the pool that afternoon. Remind your family that minimalism is about being able to live your life in a way that is more fulfilling. Consistently highlighting the benefits of minimalism, especially to your kids, will start to erode some of the resistance they may have to the idea at first. They'll eventually come to see that there even though they may have lost some of their toys, they've gained a lot of time and a lot of happiness because of minimalism.

Be a role model for them

One of the best ways to teach anything in life is to model it. So if you find that your family members just simply are not interested in this whole minimalism journey, I think the best way you can convince them to jump on board is simply to show them what it looks like and how much simpler it can make your life. I know it's easy to get down and frustrated when the people you love don't support you in your vision for your family's life. It's easy to blame them when you want to have a simpler life, but their bedroom is still full of clutter and junk and is always dirty. But try to simply do your best, declutter the areas that won't affect them, and enjoy those spaces. Let them see what a minimalist lifestyle can look like and how much happier it makes you. A lot of the time, your family will see how much less stressed you are and how much time you have, and they'll be interested just because of your example.

Don't chuck someone else's stuff.

Whatever you do, don't just start chunking everything out, regardless of whose it is. Sure, sure, you may have bought that toy, so technically, yes, it's yours. But your child won't see it that way. That toy is his. There is no faster way to squash whatever enthusiasm was starting to build than to throw out someone else's belongings. It's a hostile thing to do, and it will make your family members upset. Rightfully so. They have a right to their feelings. They have a right to be part of the process, so respect that.

Of course, there will be times that you have to set guidelines. For example, when you are going through your 8-year old's room, you might designate a specific area that can contain toys and anything that doesn't fit in that specific area. That's ok. You're still allowing them the independence to figure out what can fit in that space and make a decision about what will need to go. You're still giving them a choice about what toys they want to keep and which ones they want to give up.

It's a respect thing. You probably wouldn't like it if someone just started throwing out everything you own. Don't force minimalism on anyone. Sure, it's kind of hard to be a minimalist if no one else in your family wants to live that way but do your best. Continue to maintain your minimalist lifestyle as best as you can in your own spaces, with your own stuff, and model how much it helps you.

If you try to force it on your family, minimalism will not last. People don't just make these life changes because someone else tells them to do it. They do it because they really are behind it and they believe in it. So, if you really want to have a sustainable lifestyle change, you need to focus on the long game, model minimalism for your family, and just be patient with them.

CHAPTER 12
Recap

Who reading this has money problems? Raise your hand. It's fine. The person sitting behind you in the coffee shop isn't going to care. If you didn't raise your hand, I'm pretty sure you're lying. Because we all have money problems. Or most of us, anyway. Money is a dirty five-letter word that somehow has the power to ruin people, marriages, and even entire communities. It makes the world go around, and for some people, it can also cause the entire world to stop. It's a small word and a relatively simple concept, but it has incredible power. It's a little bit astonishing what money (or, more accurately, the desire for money) can lead people to do.

I could go on, but that's not what this book is really about. It's about you and your family and setting you up to live a minimalist lifestyle in every aspect of your life, including your finances. And guess what? In this chapter, we're going to take a deep look at what a minimalist budget can look like.

A reminder of what minimalism isn't

I don't know what you think of when you first think of the word budgeting, but for me, it makes me think "tight." It makes me think of the phrase, "tightening our belts." It makes me think of all of the things that I can't do or won't be able to do in the coming months because I haven't saved up for it. Budgeting doesn't really sound all that great most of the time. In fact, it kind of sounds like a negative view of minimalism.

Minimalism means doing without. It means having less, which can sometimes sound scary to those of us who grew up in a capitalist society. But just like minimalism isn't only about doing with less, budgeting isn't only about doing with less. It's about living within your means. It's about learning to use what you have to live a purposeful, fulfilling life. I promise you can do it on a budget.

I know it might often seem like money is incredibly important, but it's really only one resource in our lives. There are many other resources that need to be managed and used wisely. So just like minimalism isn't about starving yourself, punishing yourself, or living without anything to make life comfortable, neither is having a minimalist budget about any of those things. Both are about figuring out exactly what you need and living within those needs instead of living to excess.

A good example of this would be deciding to buy a dryer after your old one gives out. Dryers cost a lot of money, especially if you want to get a good one that will last a long time. And you can certainly dry your clothes without a dryer. All you have to do is set up a clothesline in your backyard (if you have a backyard—in your laundry room if you don't), lug out all of your wet clothes along with a bag of clothespins, and hang them out to dry. Of course, you have to be able to know that it's not going to rain and that your clothes won't get soaked all over again.

So, technically, yes, you could do without a dryer. Does it belong in a minimalist budget, then? Well, that depends: does the drying process without a dryer sound like way too much hassle? Will it leave you prisoner to the laundry in a way that will sap your other important physical resources like time and energy? It might not cost any money to dry your laundry this way, but that doesn't make it free. So, you have to decide: is the extra time and energy spent worth the money you save by not buying a new dryer?

The Purchase

For many people, shopping is a practice of mindlessness. They go into a store and simply wander the aisles, looking for something they might want without any real plan or intention in mind. Advertisers love this kind of shopper. However, part of learning to live on a minimalist budget is learning how to become a more mindful consumer. Here are some tips to help you do just that:

Don't go shopping when you're emotional, bored, or hungry

In other words, don't go shopping when you're not on your A-game. Any other time, you'll be much more vulnerable to the work of advertising. If you're hungry, an ad for a yummy, juicy hamburger is likely to send you running to the nearest fast food restaurant. If you're frustrated because your kids' clothes are already starting to get too small, an ad for the latest trends in children's clothing will tempt you to head on into the clothing store. If you're bored and simply looking for a distraction, you'll wander into a retail store without any thought as to what you might need, and you could easily end up with a cart full of things you never needed in the first place.

Many of us who have grown up in Western society has been taught that problems are most easily solved when you buy something new. You will look more stylish, your status will be raised, you'll have more friends if you have the latest clothes, etc. Ads are designed to promote those kinds of messages. So, be careful not to go shopping when you are in a compromised mental state.

Go in with a plan

This is especially true for grocery shopping, though you can make a plan when you go shopping for anything, including clothes, furniture, etc. Try your hardest not to make decisions spontaneously. Build a meal plan for your family, take a look at what you have in your pantry already, and then make a list of everything you have to have in order to follow the meal plan. Everything else in the store that might tempt you can be left on the shelf.

Look at other options

If you are looking to make a bigger purchase, it's always a good idea to stop before you buy and take a few minutes, at least, to research what your other options might be. For example, if you need to buy a new computer and you have your eyes set on one, in particular, don't buy it immediately. This is even easier to accomplish with the advent of smartphones because you don't even have to leave the store to do it. You can simply take a few moments, look at the websites of a few other retailers, and see if this is truly the best option for you. You could even look into marketplaces that sell used computers or items like Craigslist or Swappa. That way, you could even end up getting exactly what you want for a much lower price because somebody has already used it.

For smaller purchases, like at the grocery store, you can still follow this guideline. Instead of grabbing the first thing on the shelf, look around a little bit to see what is cheaper or what might be on sale.

Don't get bogged down

At the same time, it's sometimes possible to spend too much time and energy looking for those other options. In a minimalist budget, that isn't good either because time is just as important a resource as money, so you should use it wisely. If you need a bag of potatoes, for example, and there are several different kinds to choose from, simply grab the cheapest one that will work for you and move on with your life. For bigger purchases, do your research, look for cheaper options, but don't spend days and days doing it. Give it a good thirty minutes or so, and move on. So, keep the other resources in your life in mind as you make your purchasing decisions. Sometimes the time it takes to do something yourself or to research other options is worth more than the money you might save. So, learn how to balance saving time and saving money.

Deciding what's important and cutting out the rest

Once again, minimalist budgeting is not about simply financial budgeting. It takes into account your other resources, like time and energy. The goal of a minimalist budget is to find a balance between needs and wants and to divide all of your resources between them effectively. Obviously, we need to be smart with the money we have and spend it responsibly. However, you should factor in your other physical resources into your budget as well.

Time

I'm not sure if you've ever thought of it quite like this, but time is actually the most unforgiving resource available to you. Money can be made, borrowed, or even stolen (probably not a great idea, though!) when things get desperate. You can always sell your house or cut down on your monthly subscriptions. Of course, there does come a time when money can simply run out, and there's not a whole lot that can be done. So, budgeting money and being smart about how you spend it is still important.

However, time is actually much less forgiving. When time passes, it's gone. There's nothing you can sell or borrow that will bring the time back. What's worse: none of us know when our time will simply be over. We can run out of it in a moment.

So, instead of starting to build your budget with money, you should start with time. Everyone has the same amount of time: 24 hours a day, seven days a week. Decide what things are most important to you and where those things should fit in your week. You might find it helpful to spend a few days or even a full week keeping track of where your time is spent. Keep a small notebook with you and write a short note every time you change activities. I know it sounds like a lot of work, and it kind of is. But if you can do it for at least a full day, it'll be extremely helpful for you to determine which activities to keep and which ones you can stop doing. You'll probably be surprised how much of your time is spent on things that don't matter to you.

It might be tempting to look at your journal when you're done and beat yourself up over the time you consistently waste on unimportant things. Resist the urge because you'll only be wasting more time. Simply acknowledge it, take a look at the things that do matter to you, and figure out how you can be doing more of those kinds of things.

Energy

The other non-monetary resource that we have to learn how to budget is our energy. We only have a finite amount of energy, and we have to learn how to use it wisely. Kind of like time, it's easy to spend energy on things that don't really matter that much to you. I know I spend an inordinate amount of my time and energy cleaning our house. There's not really a whole lot I can do about that except to learn to be ok when things aren't exactly perfect in my home. At some point, the house does have to be clean. It does have to be safe for my family to live in, so I can't just let it go forever.

However, I could learn how to understand that life is a little messy sometimes and let my kids' toys stay in the living room until our nightly clean-up time instead of trying to pick up after them throughout the day constantly. Cleaning like that only saps the energy I should have used to play with them or to take care of other things that are important to me. After a day of cleaning up after every single mess my kids make, I'm way too tired to do things like connecting with my husband when he gets home from work or enjoying a meal with my family at the dinner table.

When you start thinking about all of the things you do throughout the day, take note of the unimportant things that sap a lot of your energy and try to figure out how you can lessen the toll it takes.

Creating your budget

Once you've identified and set apart the things in your life that are non-negotiable, you can start taking a look at the things you can move around. It's a pretty simple principle: if it's not one of your non-negotiables, find a way to either reduce the resources you spend on it or get rid of it altogether. For me, one of my non-negotiables is playing with my kids and making time for them. Constantly fussing over how clean the house is throughout the day gets in the way of that. So, I have to learn how to be ok with a bit of a mess during this phase of my life. The mess can wait, but my kids won't always be little and want me to play with them.

The same principle goes for the items you spend your money on. When creating your budget, you don't have to trim it down to the bare minimum you need to survive and save every penny over that. Not only is that not practical, but it's also unenjoyable. If you enjoy traveling, set aside a little bit of money every month to save up so that you can take a trip every few months or so. If you really love books, it's ok to spend a portion of your money on books. However, if you find that you spend a lot of money every month on things that don't matter to you, stop paying for it! Of course, be responsible! If you're in debt, you can't really decide that paying off your debt doesn't matter to you and then just stop paying for it. That's a good way to get in trouble with your credit! But, if you find that you're spending close to $100 on television services when you know, you'd really rather be out walking with your family, cancel the services! Do everything you can to spend your money on things that truly matter to you.

Creating a minimalist budget isn't nearly as scary as you might think. It's not about living on the bare minimum and saving every penny you possibly can for that future "rainy day." It's about taking all of your resources into account and spending your money on things that will serve you and your values. I strongly encourage you to consider building your budget with this mindset because I think you'll find that your entire life is more well-rounded and enjoyable.

CHAPTER 13
Reasons And Guidelines

Yay! If you've made it through to this chapter, you've at least started decluttering your home. Your family at least knows what your plans are (and hopefully, they're on board). You've set some guidelines for the items in your home and have determined why you're doing this.

Now it's time to start thinking about how you're going to maintain your new minimalist lifestyle, and unfortunately, this is the hardest part of the whole deal. It's incredibly easy for clutter to make its way back into your life. In fact, I can promise you that no matter how hard you try, it will happen. Minimalism won't keep the clutter away, but it will give you the tools you need to know how to deal with it. And giving yourself a clean slate by decluttering your house at the start will make the clutter-creep much more manageable.

The problem is, you have to be consistent about maintaining it, which can be difficult to do. If you let it go for very long, clutter has a sneaky way of accumulating rather quickly, and before you know it, you could end up with another mess on your hands.

The good news is, it can be done if you work to develop good habits and routines that will help you and your family keep your home clutter-free. Here are some tips for making that happen.

Remember why you are doing this

As always, keep your reason for doing this at the front of your family's mind. You could even write it out and put it somewhere where it will be visible to everyone in your home. If you're intentional about remembering why you want to have a minimalist lifestyle in the first place, it will be easier to find the motivation to maintain it for the long haul.

Make your house guidelines clear and visible

Just like your reason for doing this should be visible to everyone, the guidelines for your home should be visible as well. When something new comes into your home, you can hold it up against the guidelines to determine if it can stay or if it should find a new home. This also makes sure that everyone in the family knows and is clear on what the guidelines are. If you have young kids, take time to review the guidelines often to help them remember what they are and why your family has them.

Ask questions of everything you buy

Every time you go to buy something new, take a few minutes to ask yourself a few questions:
- Will I want this next month?
- Do I need this?
- Will it bring me joy?
- Can it replace something I already have?
- Am I willing to get rid of something else in order to have this?

Train your children to ask these questions, too. Maybe even add one more to it: would they be willing to spend their own money on it? Learning to ask these questions consistently will cut down dramatically on the number of new gadgets and toys you ultimately decide to buy. And you can be sure that the ones you do decide to buy will be used and enjoyed.

Make space for things that will leave

Somewhere in your home, ideally where it will be easily accessible to everyone in the family, room set a box out where people can place the things they no longer need or want. That way, as they come across the things they want to get rid of, they can immediately get it out of their home, instead of deciding to wait until they have time to decide what to do with it. Taking away that extra layer of effort will definitely help them (and you) maintain a decluttered home.

Sweep through your house every day

At the end of each day, do a quick sweep through your house to put everything back where it belongs. Have your family members join you by picking up their own belongings and returning them to their proper place. Your home doesn't have to be perfectly picked up at every moment throughout the day, but it does help to go to bed with a picked up home so that you can wake up with a clean slate for the next day.

Don't stock up on things

I know this might sound counterintuitive. Stocking up sounds like a good idea, especially when the items are necessary, and the price is low. It's hard to pass up on a really good deal! The issue is, if you stock up on things too much, they can start accumulating and will only get lost in a house that is way too full. Again, minimalism isn't just about saving every penny you possibly can. It's about learning how to live in a way that is fulfilling and that you honestly enjoy. If coupon-clipping and stocking up on sale items only lead to more stress and clutter, don't do it! Save money by buying the off-brand laundry detergent or whatever the item is.

Learn how to borrow

Sometimes you'll have an item in your home that serves a purpose that can't really be duplicated by another item but that you only use on rare occasions. If you know someone who also owns the item, it might be possible for you to get rid of yours and simply borrow theirs on the rare occasions you need it. There's no sense in you storing an item that is only used once in a blue moon, so try to see what items you can borrow from someone else.

Get rid of the clutter magnets

Some items in your house are just magnets for clutter. Keeping extra storage containers, for example, is just asking for them to be filled with new forms of clutter. It never fails: an empty, purposeless drawer will eventually become filled. If you have a desk or table that always seems to be covered in clutter, would it be better for you to just do without that piece of furniture? If you can get by without it, do it. Simply don't allow yourself or your family a place for clutter to accumulate.

Limit the number of possessions your family can have

If you and your family struggle to control the number of possessions you have, it might be a good idea to set a limit on yourselves. Count your possessions from time to time to see if you've exceeded your limit. If you have, it's time to cut back on a few of your possessions. I wouldn't be super strict about this. Counting your possessions every single day can be an unnecessary and draining task that will only bring frustration and conflict. However, doing it from time to time can be a good, objective way to determine if your family has too much stuff.

Stop going shopping

For a time, at least, set a ban on shopping. Decide what the essentials are that you will continue to buy and then simply stop buying anything that doesn't fall into that essential category. Items like food and toiletries will still have to be bought, but clothes, books, movies, etc. can all wait until the ban is over. This is a good way to give your budget a bit of a break as well as your newly-decluttered home.

Stick with your community

Hopefully, by this point in your journey, your family members have all decided to jump on board with you. If that's the case, you might not feel like you need a community of like-minded people you joined back when you were on your own in the minimalism journey. You may have since found the support and encouragement you needed then, but it's still a great idea to stay in touch with the people who helped you at the beginning of the journey. They'll continue to be another source of encouragement and accountability as you work to maintain the habits of minimalism. They'll help you stay motivated when the going gets tough. So, stay connected to the online communities and blogs and continue to educate yourself about minimalism and strategies for continuing on the journey.

Resist the temptation to make impulse purchases

Every time you go shopping, you're at risk of making an impulse purchase. Advertising companies and retailers spend inordinate amounts of money on ads designed to convince us to buy things we really know we could do without. And they're really, really good at it. They're so good, you often won't even realize you bought into the ad's promises until you turn around and the purchase is made. I've said it before, but I'll say it again: always go into a store with a plan. Have your grocery list, your list of clothing needs, etc. in hand any time you walk into a store. If you come across something you think you need/want that isn't on your list, write it down and walk away. When you're finished shopping, think about it again: is it really worth going back and finding it again now that you're done shopping, or would you rather check out and go home? If the answer is yes, it's worth it, go for it. If the answer is no, I'd rather just be done, then great! Either way, you resisted making a purchase on impulse by giving yourself time to think about it and get over the initial excitement of it.

Declutter your schedule

I know it's hard to do, especially if you have kids in school, a full-time job, and everything else going on in the world. However, minimalism doesn't work well with a busy life. You'll find yourself constantly running and never taking the time to follow through on the habits you're trying to build. It's hard to be consistent about following your family's guidelines when everyone's too busy. Decide what's absolutely necessary and worth the time and energy and simply stop doing all the rest.

Set goals with your family

Work with your family members to set goals for your home. If you and your family can have a specific and appealing goal in mind, it will make it that much easier for everyone to stay motivated. Plan a family vacation after your home has been fully decluttered. Or pay off as much debt as possible with the money you save during a shopping ban. Making goals that your entire family can get behind will help motivate them to continue.

Practice thankfulness

When we learn how to be thankful for the things we have in our lives and in our homes, it makes it much easier for us to resist the urge to accumulate more. If you already believe you have enough and are thankful for everything you have, you won't feel the lack that leads to impulsive purchasing decisions and clutter-creep. Institute a daily moment of thanks with your family. Take a few minutes every day, whether it's at bedtime, at the dinner table, or as you drive your kids to school every morning, to talk about everything you're thankful for. Have your kids do the same. If they're not sure where to start, have them come up with at least three things in their life that they're thankful for.

It can be simple things, and, in the beginning, you might even allow repeats. However, as you and your family get in the habit of saying what you're thankful for, tighten up the ropes a little bit. Everyone has to come up with something unique and thoughtful. Three of your kids can't say "I'm thankful for my family" every day. That's cheating. If they get stuck, you might prompt them to think about why they're thankful for their family or what specific person they're thankful for at that moment. Teaching your kids how to be truly thankful for everything in their lives will be a great lesson for them to learn, not only during their years in your minimalist home but throughout their entire lives.

A note about gifts

One of the most difficult parts about living a minimalist lifestyle is what to do about gift-giving holidays. It doesn't matter if your family is just starting out on the journey or if you're old pros at it and have lived this way for a while. Gift-giving holidays can present a unique set of challenges that you'll have to learn how to best navigate for your family.

A minimalist mindset and holidays

Holidays and birthdays can be tough. I don't know about you, but it kind of hurts me to think of my kids not getting gifts around the holidays. It's silly and honestly a little bit dumb, I know, but I remember having so much fun around Christmas and my birthday as a kid, trying to guess what new treasures I would get and then ripping open the wrapping paper to see if I was right. And it's kind of difficult to think about not letting my kids have that experience.

However, if I take off my rose-colored glasses and look at my childhood experience objectively, I remember actually feeling disappointed at the end of the gift-giving segment of the day. I would have all of my brand-new toys sitting all around me, but I would already have a countdown running in my mind for the next holiday. Mind you, gifts are not bad things, and I promise I wasn't an abnormally ungrateful, self-centered kid. I was simply a normal kid growing up in Western society. I may have been normal, but that doesn't mean it was the best experience or that I was right for feeling that way. And it doesn't mean that I want my own kids to grow up with those kinds of expectations and attitudes.

Instead, I would like for my kids to have the experiences and memories that truly important and meaningful in my own childhood. Those memories weren't about the gifts I received; they were about the family I got to be around. They were about the traditions of my faith that surround the holiday. They were about being reminded that my family loves, values, and celebrates the day I was born. So, I would encourage you to adopt a mindset around holidays that puts the focus back on the true meaning of it instead of what kind of new, cool toys and gadgets your kids will be getting.

Unfortunately, not everyone in your family will understand why you want to limit (or even completely stop) the gift-exchange tradition. I know my own parents love to give my kids gifts, and they weren't very thrilled when I told them I didn't want them to buy any more toys for my boys. However, you simply have to stand firm. Give your extended family ample notice, especially if they tend to buy gifts throughout the year as sales arise or they find something they think will be particularly enjoyed. If your extended family really wants to buy something, have them give you and your kids' experiences. Tickets to a baseball game or a concert might be a great idea. It's true that holidays can be a little tricky to navigate with extended family members, but I promise it can be done, and you'll be glad you did it.

By working with your family to learn the habits of minimalism, you'll eventually come to find that it's not that difficult to maintain. Simply stay mindful, stay consistent, and stay patient with yourself and everyone in your family. Easier said than done, I know! But believe me, it's definitely worth the initial struggle!

CONCLUSION

Thank you for making it through to the end of Minimalism for Families. I really hope it was informative and was able to provide you with all of the tools you need to achieve your goals, whatever they may be.

In this book, we discussed everything you need to know to develop a mindset of minimalism and build a minimalist lifestyle your entire family can follow. First, we talked about what minimalism is and what it can look like in the life of an entire family. We went through specific strategies for explaining minimalism to your family members and convincing them to jump on board. We talked about methods you can use to declutter your home, as well as specific tips and tricks for each room in your house. Finally, we talked about how to deal with family members who remain unconvinced and resistant to your vision of minimalism, as well as how to maintain a lifestyle of minimalism for the long-haul.

I hope this book was extremely practical and useful to you and that it provided you with much-needed encouragement and motivation along the way. As I'm sure you discovered throughout the pages of this book, minimalism is an incredibly worthwhile mindset and lifestyle. It will help you and your family learn how to focus on the things that truly matter in your life, like spending more time with each other. It might be a bit painful and difficult at first, but I'm willing to bet that your entire family will eventually come to see the value of it.

As you went through the pages of this book, I hope you kept in mind that the guidelines I have written out here are only the opinion of one person. I obviously do not know you or your family. Feel free to take the tips and ideas I've outlined and adjusted it to fit the needs of your family.

The next step is to get started developing a mindset of minimalism in your family and building a minimalist lifestyle that you can all follow! Purchasing and reading this book was a great start toward that goal, but now it's up to you to take what you learned here and use it. Throughout this book, I tried to provide a step-by-step process that's easy to follow so you can use this book as a guide for developing a minimalist mindset and building a lifestyle of minimalism.

Finally, if you found this book useful in any way, a review on Amazon is always appreciated!

DESCRIPTION

When you think of Minimalism, what comes to mind? It is worth noting that minimalism is about trading all of the excess junk that piles up so easily for more of what brings me joy: spending time with my family and friends, writing, sleeping, and experiencing life. It's about teaching my kids to live simple lives so that we can experience the beauty of the world together. It's about working with my husband to build the life we want for our family instead of fighting with him about all of the junk that needs to be taken care of.

One of the aspects worth noting is that in order to start on the journey to minimalism is how to ask the right questions. If you haven't done it already, you should seriously stop reading right now and take a few minutes to consider your reasons for doing this, as well as the purpose you want your family and your home to have.

In other words, Minimalism is a mindset and a lifestyle. It's not a project to be completed in a weekend and put back on the shelf for next time. It's a chance to reconsider what your priorities are and to design your life (and your stuff) around those priorities. And although minimalism usually starts by getting rid of excess physical clutter.

It is worth noting that minimalism involves a lot of issues that are relevant in life. For instance, It might seem ridiculous to think that minimalism can actually work for an entire family—especially one with a couple of young kids. Between all of the sports gear—participating in multiple sports at a time builds character, right? —clothes, school supplies, and toys that constantly pile up, cutting it all down to only the things that are necessary (and keeping it that way) seem an impossible task. Thus, you need to create some more time and grasp some more aspects of minimalism.

In a nutshell, in this book you'll learn:
- What is minimalism?
- Advantages of having a minimalist lifestyle
- Developing a mindset of minimalism
- Strategies for the cleanup
- Aspect on:
    1. Furniture
    2. Bookshelves
    3. Decorations
    4. Coffee Tables
    5. Electronics
    6. Sentimental items
    7. Special spaces for the kids
- You need to create some more time and learn more on:

1. The Beauty of Humanity
2. Find your people
3. Remind them of the benefits
4. Be a role model for them
5. Don't chuck someone else's stuff.

You will also have a golden chance of understanding why minimalism is a trade. In that, like I said earlier, minimalism isn't about setting unrealistic limits on what you can own. It's about making a trade. Everything costs something, so when you choose to accept something into your life, you're also choosing to let go of something else.

www.ingramcontent.com/pod-product-compliance
Lightning Source LLC
Chambersburg PA
CBHW071407070526
44578CB00002B/504